THE BATTLE OF
NEW MARKET HEIGHTS

THE BATTLE OF
NEW MARKET HEIGHTS

FREEDOM WILL BE THEIRS BY THE SWORD

JAMES S. PRICE

FOREWORD BY O. JAMES LIGHTHIZER, PRESIDENT OF THE CIVIL WAR TRUST

SERIES EDITOR DOUGLAS BOSTICK

Charleston   London

THE
History
PRESS

Published by The History Press
Charleston, SC 29403
www.historypress.net

First published 2011

Manufactured in the United States

ISBN 978.1.60949.038.6

Price, James S.
The Battle of New Market Heights : freedom will be theirs by the sword / James S. Price.
p. cm.
Includes bibliographical references and index.
ISBN 978-1-60949-038-6
1. New Market Heights, Battle of, Va., 1864. 2. United States--History--Civil War,
1861-1865--Participation, African American. 3. United States. Army--African American
troops--History--19th century. I. Title.
E477.21.P74 2011
973.7'415--dc23
2011029003

CONTENTS

FOREWORD

B y September 1864, the Union army was mired in the trenches of Petersburg, locked in a desperate struggle that would ultimately decide the fate of a nation. The war had taken a long and circuitous route to reach this spot in Virginia, preceded by a string of bloody campaigns marked with crushing defeats for both Union and Confederate armies alike.

The casualty figures that rocked the nation in 1862 at Sharpsburg and Shiloh were followed by the frightening bloodshed of 1863 at places like Chancellorsville, Gettysburg and Chickamauga—sites on the map that are still synonymous today with tremendous suffering. In 1864, the landscape ran brilliantly red with the living crimson of Americans both North and South as the Union army launched headlong into the heart of Virginia, the very nature of the war shifting with the unceasing pressure of the onslaught.

Beginning with the Overland Campaign, the Civil War wrought casualties and destruction heretofore thought impossible. It was suffering and loss on the grandest of scales for both armies. And for the mud-spattered private in either army, it seemed that there might never be an end to this bloody struggle. Desperation, misery and gloom were indeed the watchwords of this tragic chapter of American history.

During this hour of unending despair, black soldiers also launched a heroic and successful attack and, in doing so, changed the course of our history. For far too long, their story has gone largely untold, but in Jimmy Price's *The Battle of New Market Heights: Freedom Will Be Theirs by the Sword,* these brave soldiers have finally received a testament worthy of their valor—a recognition in ink for their brave deeds in the field. Now, thanks to Mr. Price's diligent research, students of the war finally have a volume that details one of the most important, if not *the* most important, moments in United States African American military history.

Frederick Douglass famously offered that "[o]nce let the black man get upon his person the brass letter, U.S., let him get an eagle on his button, and a musket on his shoulder and bullets in his pocket, there is no power on earth that can deny that he has earned the right to citizenship." In the work that follows, we now have certifiable and unquestionable evidence of the veracity of Mr. Douglass's estimation of the import of enlisting black soldiers. This is a story worth remembering, a story that had been largely lost—often relegated to the dusty footnote of most major campaign histories.

As a lifelong preservationist and president of a group concerned about the future of the battlefields on which this war was decided, I am exceedingly thankful for the publication of this volume. Simply put: good history begets good preservation. And for those working to save these now deathless fields, this work will provide an excellent framework for preservationists to utilize as they rally to save the ground on which these soldiers gained their laurels and on which our collective American history was written.

To date, precious few acres of the New Market Heights battlefield have been saved, but it is my earnest hope that this will change over the next four years of the sesquicentennial commemoration, and if it does, we have historians like Mr. Price to thank for his work in creating a dialogue about this important moment in history. As we move through the commemoration, I can only hope that more historians follow his lead and use this unique opportunity to reexamine our history with fresh eyes, calling attention to episodes and personalities not previously given their due.

O. James Lighthizer
Washington, D.C.
May 31, 2011

PREFACE

Thursday, September 29, 1864, is arguably one of the most important days in American history. Without question, it is certainly one of the most (if not *the* most) important days in African American military history. On that day, in a few short hours of bloody fighting, the Federal Army of the James broke the outer ring of defenses protecting the Confederate capital of Richmond, Virginia. And at a place called New Market Heights, where a line of defenses was built to protect one of the vital inroads to that city, one of the most elite units in Robert E. Lee's vaunted Army of Northern Virginia was dislodged from its trenches by Union troops.

But these weren't just any Union troops; these were black soldiers of the United States Colored Troops (USCT). Despised by Confederates and shunned by many whites in their own army, these African American soldiers had much to prove and even more to gain on that fateful day. Their nearly suicidal charge against strong defenses manned by veteran troops who were incensed at the sight of blacks in uniform could have been disastrous had it failed. The whole race would have shouldered the burden, and the hopes of freedom, equality and citizenship could have been deferred if not altogether abandoned had the Union experiment in arming blacks and letting them strike a blow for their own freedom resulted in ignominious failure. Indeed, many white Northerners in the Union army viewed blacks in uniform as a misguided experiment that would prove once and for all that blacks were inferior and would scatter at the first shot that they heard fired in anger.

Just a few short weeks before this assault, Northerners were shocked to learn of the disastrous Battle of the Crater fought outside the city of Petersburg on July 30, 1864. During that battle, roughly 4,500 USCTs had fought. About 1,300 of them became casualties. Even though the majority of the black troops fought with valor and distinction at the Crater, poor leadership by the white officers in command conspired to rob the colored troops of the laurels that they deserved.

And so it came to pass that the African American soldiers who charged at New Market Heights had much riding on their shoulders. When the smoke cleared and the fighting was over, for once the black troops knew the exultant joy of driving an enemy from his position. Not only had they driven the Confederates from the field of battle, they had also "wiped out effectually the imputation against the fighting qualities of the colored troops," as the African American newspaper correspondent Thomas Morris Chester wrote after the battle.[1] Furthermore, fourteen black soldiers were awarded Congressional Medals of Honor for their heroism at New Market Heights. Major General Benjamin Franklin Butler, who commanded the Army of the James at the time of New Market Heights, thought that fourteen Medals of Honor were not enough and had his own special medal distributed to the veterans of September 29, 1864.

It finally seemed that the wrongs that African American soldiers had endured for many months had been righted. White soldiers in the Army of the James willingly (or, in many cases, begrudgingly) respected their black comrades in arms and cited New Market Heights as proof positive of their fighting prowess. At the dawn of the twentieth century, one white veteran wrote that "the story of the part taken by the colored soldiers in the war which resulted in establishing the freedom of his race will at the hands of some future historian form a romantic chapter in the history of the progress of the Republic."[2]

Unfortunately, the tragic history of race relations in the United States in the aftermath of the American Civil War ensured that the story would not be told for generations to come. Indeed, to this very day many Americans—even those with more than a passing interest in the Civil War—know next to nothing about the contributions made by black soldiers or about the battle for which fourteen of them won Medals of Honor. After the war, those trumpeting the tale of New Market Heights were the black veterans themselves.

Joseph T. Wilson, himself a veteran of the 2nd Louisiana Native Guards and the 54th Massachusetts, chronicled the tale in his 1881 book *The Black*

Phalanx: A History of the Negro Soldiers of the United States in the Wars of 1775–1812, 1861–'65. Seven years later, George W. Williams, another black veteran, wrote *A History of the Negro Troops in the War of the Rebellion, 1861–1865.* Both of these overviews include the fighting at New Market Heights, but both are incomplete. Wilson relies on newspaper accounts and after-action reports to tell the story. Williams's account is a bit more problematic, since he confuses the fighting at New Market Heights with the fighting at Fort Harrison.[3]

In addition to the veterans themselves, Benjamin Butler did much to promote the heroism of his black soldiers—as well as his role in their rise to prominence. Butler later claimed that after witnessing the bravery of the black troops and the carnage left in the aftermath of their assault, he swore to himself "an oath, which I hope and believe I have kept sacredly, that they and their race should be cared for and protected by me to the extent of my power so long as I lived."[4] Butler was true to his word and regaled his fellow congressmen with the story of New Market Heights during the heated debate over what would become the Civil Rights Act of 1875, which was ruled to be unconstitutional in 1883.

Nonetheless, as time dragged on and the mood of the country turned toward reconciliation and reunification, the story of emancipation and black military service slowly eroded from public memory of the Civil War. As a result, the story of New Market Heights all but vanished from the record until 1981, when Richard J. Sommers published *Richmond Redeemed: The Siege at Petersburg.* In a magisterial military history, Sommers examined the clash at New Market Heights within the larger framework of Grant's Fifth Offensive during the Richmond-Petersburg Campaign. Thus, only one chapter of a 670-page book describes the battle. It would not be until 2004 that another author would give an accounting of the events of September 29, 1864. Dr. Louis H. Manarin's massive two-volume *Henrico County: Field of Honor* devotes a chapter to New Market Heights in what is, by far, the most complete retelling of the battle that has yet been written.

Similarly, in the years since the motion picture *Glory* was released, public interest in the involvement of Unites States Colored Troops has increased, and several general works have been written that give an overall history of black service during the Civil War. Dudley Taylor Cornish's *The Sable Arm: Negro Troops in the Union Army 1861–1865* (1956) paved the way for future studies like Joseph T. Glatthaar's *Forged in Battle: The Civil War Alliance of Black Soldiers and White Officers* (1990) and Noah Andre Trudeau's *Like Men of War: Black Troops in the Civil War 1862–1865* (1998). These books helped to generate more specialized works and fuel interest in individual tales of black heroism. This led to 2005's *Uncommon Valor: A Story of Race, Patriotism, and Glory in the Final Battles of the Civil War* by Melvin Claxton and Mark Puls. This monograph focuses on Christian Fleetwood and several of his compatriots who were awarded Medals of Honor for the fighting at New Market Heights and recounts the story of the battle from the perspective of the black troops. The book was designed for general audiences and, once again, only devotes one chapter to the battle proper.

Thus, while the groundwork has been laid for an overall history of the Battle of New Market Heights, a general synthesis of these disparate sources into one narrative is necessary as the sesquicentennial commemoration of the American Civil War gets underway. It is my hope that this book will be the starting point for all who wish to further their understanding of the contributions of black troops, as well as how that contribution was brought into stunning clarity in the trenches of New Market Heights.

As is the case with any historical work, the list of people to whom I owe thanks would take up half of the following pages if I were to name them all. However, a few individuals must be named for helping to bring this project to fruition.

Hannah Cassilly, my editor at The History Press, initiated this project and walked me through the entire process, patiently answering questions along the way. I consider it a high honor that this volume will stand alongside the other excellent books in the Civil War Sesquicentennial Series.

Mike Andrus, who for many years compiled information on New Market Heights while working at Richmond National Battlefield Park, was kind enough to share his extensive knowledge of the battle and take the time to walk over the battlefield with me several times. Although Mike has retired, two current members of the RNB staff—Ed Sanders and Robert E.L. Krick—were kind enough to accommodate me and allow me to access the invaluable files that the park possesses.

Many thanks to Rob Lyon for kindly allowing me to use his rare photographs of Milton Holland and Joseph Scroggs. The Maryland Historical Society also granted me permission to use the image of the 4th United States Colored Troop's flag, for which I am extremely grateful.

Jim Lighthizer, president of the Civil War Trust, graciously agreed to write the foreword for this volume, and it is my sincere hope that the following pages will help preserve what is left of the New Market Heights battlefield for future generations. Rob Shenk at the CWT was also a believer in this project, and I thank him for helping to spread the word about this book.

Master cartographer Steven Stanley was able to take my clumsy descriptions of troop movements and battlefield maneuvers and turn them into a beautiful set of maps. I count myself fortunate to include his excellent work in my first book.

I would also like to thank everyone who takes the time to read my weblog, The Sable Arm: A Blog Dedicated to the United States Colored Troops of the Civil War Era. This book literally would not exist if it weren't for people spreading the word about this pet project of mine, and I have been humbled by everyone who has read my posts since its inception.

Last but not least, I would like to thank my lovely wife, Gina, for enduring my bouts of insanity while I was trying to complete this manuscript. She jokingly refers to me as a "Civil War extremist," and those words were never truer than when I was wrestling with the events of September 29, 1864. Her love and support brought me through to the other side, and I owe her a debt that could never be expressed in words alone.

Soli Deo gloria.

Chapter 1

"THE OBJECT...IS TO SURPRISE AND CAPTURE RICHMOND"

FALL OF 1864

In the predawn darkness of Thursday, September 29, 1864, a blue-clad host was preparing to attack a strong line of Confederate entrenchments. As the officers got the men into line, cartridge boxes were shifted forward for easier access, and cap pouches were fingered nervously, although the men were under strict orders not to cap their loaded muskets. At this late stage in the war, officers had learned that the distance between an attacking column and its objective needed to be covered as quickly as possible—men stopping to fire their muskets would slow down the advancing foot soldiers and expose their comrades to murderous fire from the enemy position. No, this line of Rebel trenches would have to be taken with sheer grit, determination and the point of the bayonet.

If all went according to plan and the Confederates were driven from their works, the prize that awaited these men was none other than the capital of the Confederate States of America: Richmond, Virginia. The city that had come to symbolize all of the frustration that had plagued the Union army in Virginia ever since the heady days of 1862 was finally within reach. All that needed to happen was for these troops to take it.

As one Yankee officer later recalled:

> *I know that there was a big lot of thinking done by us while we stood there. We knew there was a strong line of Confederates behind the rifle pits...We knew that as soon as we would move forward they would open fire on us. We knew that the order to go forward would soon be given. But beyond that what? Would it be death, or wounds, or capture? Would it be victory or defeat?*[5]

Speed was the key. Once the order to attack was given, the men would have to step off at a quick pace and let momentum carry them up to the brink of the rifle pits. They knew that the Confederates had strewn the earth in front of their trenches with various obstacles that would have to be cleared away as quickly as possible. While the obstructions were being cleared, the attacking soldiers would have to wait and endure the punishing musket and artillery fire that would rake their lines. In short, no one suffered from any delusions that this would be a quick and easy victory. Each man had to steel himself for what he was about to experience and for what might be waiting for him on the other side of the enemy's trenches.

All of these concerns were typical for any attacking force on either side during the American Civil War. Fear of wounds and death knew no distinctions between blue and gray. Fear of being captured and sent to one of the infamous prison camps, like Andersonville or Libby Prison, was a running concern as well. However, for the Union soldiers forming at the edge of the obstructions, what would happen in the event that they were taken prisoner was even more disquieting than usual.

These men belonged to Colonel Samuel A. Duncan's 3rd Brigade of Brigadier General Charles J. Paine's 3rd Division of the 18th Corps, Army of the James. Duncan commanded just two regiments that morning: the 4th and 6th USCT. The warriors who would be storming the trenches that morning were African American enlisted men commanded by white officers, and the Confederates who were dug in just a few hundred yards away held these soldiers in special contempt. Before the Civil War had started, many white Southerners had very legitimate fears of their slaves rising up and fighting for their freedom—the United States Colored Troops represented the realization of that fear. Not only were the Rebel soldiers incensed to see blacks in uniform, they were also fighting with their backs against their nation's capital. They would not yield without a fight. Duncan's troops knew this, and yet when the order to advance was given at about 5:30 a.m., they stepped off without hesitation. Before them loomed New Market Heights.

The chain of events leading up to the Battle of New Market Heights can be traced back to March 1864, when Ulysses S. Grant was awarded the rank of lieutenant general and was given command of all Union armies. Grant wasted no time in trying to bring the war in the East to a speedy conclusion, unleashing an offensive in May designed to crush the Confederate war effort in Virginia. As Grant later recalled:

"The Object...Is to Surprise and Capture Richmond"

My general plan now was to concentrate all the force possible against the Confederate armies in the field...Accordingly I arranged for a simultaneous movement all along the line...[Major General Franz] *Sigel was in command in the Valley of Virginia. He was to advance up the valley, covering the North from an invasion through that channel as well while advancing as by remaining near Harpers Ferry...*[Major General Benjamin F.] *Butler was to advance by the James River, having Richmond and Petersburg as his objective.*[6]

While these two efforts were taking place, Grant would make his headquarters with Major General George Gordon Meade's Army of the Potomac. With Lee's supply lines being cut off by Sigel's and Butler's operations, the Army of the Potomac would deliver the fatal blow by going up against Robert E. Lee's vaunted Army of Northern Virginia. After crossing the Rapidan River, Meade's force had two goals: inflict as much damage on Lee's army as possible and surprise and capture the Rebel capital at Richmond. Grant left no mystery, however, as to which of these goals ranked highest. In his orders to Meade, Grant stated bluntly: "Lee's army will be your objective point. Wherever Lee goes, there you will go also."[7] It was readily apparent that things were going to be managed differently with Grant in charge.

After the Federals had crossed the Rapidan River on May 4, 1864, Grant decided to push his men speedily through a dense and uninhabitable region filled with scrub brush and thickets known as the Wilderness. And it was there, on May 5 and 6, that the first brutal meeting between the opposing armies' foremost commanders took place. Following the Wilderness, a series of bloody battles ensued all the way up to final assaults at Cold Harbor on June 3, 1864. The end result was more than fifty-five thousand casualties for the Union forces. This was bloodletting on a scale unimaginable, but the Federals were knocking at the gates of Richmond.[8]

Even though Grant had pushed Lee back to the outskirts of the Rebel capital, morale on the Northern homefront was sagging and, in some places, nonexistent. The summer of 1864 bore witness to the nadir of public support and enthusiasm for the Union war effort. Antiwar politicians combined with pro-Confederate "Copperheads" to stir up outrage among a Northern public that had been asked to support a conflict that had dragged on longer than anyone had expected and had cost tens of thousands of their sons.

The year 1864 was also a crucial one regarding the presidential election, and the Democratic National Convention nominated none other than

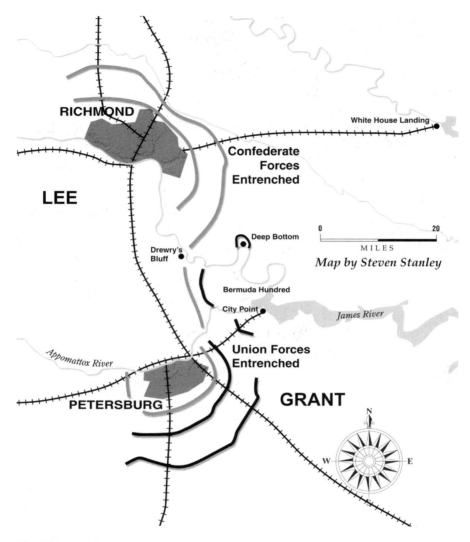

The Richmond-Petersburg front, 1864. *Steven Stanley, cartographer.*

George Brinton McClellan as its candidate to challenge Lincoln for the White House. McClellan still enjoyed a loyal following among his former soldiers in the Army of the Potomac and was an appealing prowar candidate. As the summer of 1864 wore on, the price of gold skyrocketed as speculators began to bet against a Federal victory and, by insinuation, a second term for Abraham Lincoln.

"The Object...Is to Surprise and Capture Richmond"

Lincoln's hopes were further deflated when Lee detached his 2nd Corps under the command of Major General Jubal Early for independent operations in the Shenandoah Valley in mid-June. Early was a capable officer with an excellent record up to this point, and he carried out a successful month-long campaign to counter the advance of Major General David Hunter's forces up the valley. From June 18 to July 9, 1864, Early pieced together an impressive string of victories that culminated with his secessionist hosts reaching the outskirts of Washington, D.C., on July 11. Following this humiliation, the noted New York lawyer, diarist and founder of the United States Sanitary Commission, George Templeton Strong, confided in his diary that "I see no bright spot anywhere… [only] humiliation and disaster." Strong glumly concluded, "The blood and treasure spent on this summer's campaign have done little for the country." Strong was by no means alone in his sentiments.[9]

To face the threat posed by Early's Confederates, Grant was forced to rush the 6th Corps of the Army of the Potomac up to the Shenandoah Valley via train so that Lincoln—who had seen the Rebels with his own eyes from the parapets of Fort Stevens in the nation's capital—could be assured that the capital would not fall. Northern morale had dropped even further because of Early's march to the gates of Washington. Something had to be done.

In order to swat Early far enough away from Washington for Lincoln and the Northern public to be satisfied, Grant summoned one of his old subordinates from the western theater: fiery young Philip H. Sheridan. After naming Sheridan to command the new Army of the Shenandoah, Grant ordered him to attack Early and lay waste to the agricultural assets of the valley itself. Farmers in the valley supplied the men of Lee's army, and the Shenandoah was rightly called the "breadbasket of the Confederacy."

While events quickly unfolded in the valley, it became clear that Lincoln needed to have his controversial policies—especially that of emancipation—vindicated on the field of battle. If this did not occur, the presidency and the course of the war could change in a matter of weeks. Lincoln was quite cognizant of this fact, as he remarked to a friend in August 1864, "You think I don't know I am going to be beaten, but I do, and unless some great change takes place, badly beaten."[10] While many viewed the capture of Atlanta as the overall turning point in the presidential election of 1864, Lincoln still needed a vindication of the Emancipation Proclamation and the recruitment of blacks into the army and navy.

Lucky for Lincoln, Sheridan struck a telling blow against Early's Confederate troops at the Third Battle of Winchester on September 19. On the twenty-second, "Little Phil" won another victory at Fisher's Hill that forced Early to retreat and abandon a portion of the valley, leaving it at the mercy of Sheridan's soldiers. Lee quickly tried to reinforce his troops in the valley and hoped that the reinforcements would arrive unnoticed. However, through the efforts of two of the most polarizing and controversial characters the Union ever produced, Grant knew the comings and goings of Rebel forces almost as well as Lee himself. Thanks to Elizabeth Van Lew—a Union sympathizer who ran an underground spy network in the Confederate capital—and Major General Benjamin F. Butler, Grant was supplied with a steady stream of vital and accurate military intelligence.[11]

Elizabeth Van Lew was born in the city of Richmond in 1818 and belonged to an upper crust family who lived in one of the finest mansions in the entire city. When war broke out, her staunch loyalty to the Union exposed her to threats and peeved her Rebel neighbors to no end. Not only did she give aid to Union prisoners and help them escape whenever she could, she also ran one of the war's most successful spy rings, going so far as to plant a spy in the Confederate White House.[12]

The Van Lew spy ring had set up a series of five relay stations between Richmond and Grant's headquarters at City Point. A courier would come by the Van Lew mansion and pick up messages from Elizabeth herself. This courier would then pass these missives down through a series of relays until they reached their intended target. This system was so efficient that Grant's headquarters received, on average, three reports per week giving a wealth of information about the state of Richmond's defenses and the comings and goings of various Confederate units. It was through the Van Lew network that Grant learned of the reinforcements that Lee had sent to the valley. This crucial intelligence would free Sheridan to strike a blow against Early and spurred Grant to threaten Richmond while Lee's army was undermanned.

Because of the impressive work accomplished by Van Lew's spy ring, General Butler—a politician turned officer who had a knack for attracting controversy—made contact with her in December 1863. Butler was a skilled hand at running espionage rings, a trait he had been perfecting ever since the early days as the commander at Fort Monroe in Hampton Roads, Virginia. He had maintained spy rings in Norfolk, Portsmouth, New Orleans and Richmond. By 1864, Van Lew's network was able to report to Butler that "there was a camp of seven regiments in the neighborhood of Deep Bottom" and that the fortifications outside Richmond were being strengthened. Butler himself later recalled, "With a view of finding out how matters stood with [the Confederates] in that part of their lines, I caused my scouts and secret service men to make a most thorough investigation." With such critical information pouring in, the Federals had the advantage of knowing when and where to strike, and they would put this information to good use in late September 1864.[13]

For Robert E. Lee, the defense of the Rebel capital was becoming a logistical nightmare, and every day it seemed as though he had fewer and fewer pieces to shuffle across the chessboard of war. Not only was Lee running out of men, he was also running out of time. Lee himself had famously predicted that he and his remaining men "must destroy this army of Grant's before he gets to James River. If he gets there, it will become a siege, and then it will be a mere question of time."[14]

When the great campaign had unfolded in May, Lee had proven a wily opponent for Grant and had stymied his advances into the Wilderness. But as the Overland Campaign dragged on, the Army of Northern Virginia was repeatedly forced to shift its position to block the Federal advance. And every shift brought it slowly and methodically closer to Richmond. Like Grant, Lee's army had taken a pounding from the Wilderness to Cold Harbor—about thirty-six thousand men.[15] As the campaign moved toward Petersburg, Lee was forced to defend a series of earthworks that would eventually stretch for more than thirty miles.

As the two armies settled into a siege, Grant began a strategy of slowly lengthening his lines and cutting off the vital roads and rail lines running into Petersburg. This strategy not only choked off the supplies that Lee's army desperately needed, it also constantly increased the amount of territory that the Southerners were forced to defend. Like a rubber band being stretched to its breaking point, the time was coming when Lee's lines were going to snap. As one dejected Southerner put it, "The situation was one of simply waiting to be overwhelmed."[16]

Lee, the paragon of aggressive offensive maneuvers, was now pinned back and was forced to be reactive instead of proactive. He expressed his frustration with this predicament in a letter to President Jefferson Davis on September 2, 1864: "As matters now stand we have no troops disposable to meet movements of the enemy or strike when opportunity presents, without taking them from the trenches and exposing some important point."[17]

As the siege progressed, he proved to be adept at fending off the main blows that were sent at him, but for the moment his hopes lay in holding out long enough for a decisive victory—if not on his front then in some other sector. Over time he became transfixed with what was happening in the Shenandoah Valley—it attracted him "like a magnet; it held for him

Confederate general Braxton Bragg gained a reputation for being unlikeable that bled over to his performance on the field. His service as Jefferson Davis's strategic advisor in 1864 would win him no new admirers. *Library of Congress.*

the possibility of relieving Grant's death grip at Petersburg."[18] If Lee could tread water long enough, the South's hopes for independence might yet be achieved. Lee was fully aware of the crisis in morale that the North faced, and he knew that the presidential election could be a game changer, as long as Lincoln lost, of course.

Since Grant's main efforts were usually concentrated on the Petersburg front, Lee showed relatively little concern about the defenses north of the James River that protected Richmond itself. In July and August, the Federals had mounted offensives against this portion of the Confederate defense network and had been stymied both times. When his hands were tied with the entrenchments defending Petersburg, Lee relied on his subordinates to handle any danger that might crop up north of the James.

The officers in charge of handling affairs on the north side of the James reads like a veritable "who's who" of Confederate has-beens. Serving as the de facto general in chief and special advisor to President Davis was none other than General Braxton Bragg. Enormously unpopular in his controversial dealings in the western theater of the war, Davis brought his old friend to Richmond early in 1864, where he was "charged with the conduct of military operations in the armies of the Confederacy."[19] This meant that Bragg was superior even to Lee, who had held a similar post before being given command of the Army of Northern Virginia in June 1862.

Heading the Department of Richmond was the former commander of the Army of Northern Virginia's 2nd Corps, Lieutenant General Richard S. Ewell. "Old Bald Head," as he was known to his men, had not performed up to scratch during the Battles of the Wilderness and Spotsylvania Courthouse, and after the Overland Campaign was concluded, Lee put Jubal Early in charge of the 2nd Corps and charged Ewell with command of the Department of Richmond as of June 15, 1864.[20] Rounding out the cast of characters with checkered pasts was Lieutenant Colonel (formerly Lieutenant General) John C. Pemberton—the soldier known throughout the South as the man who surrendered Vicksburg, Mississippi, to the Yankees in July 1863.

These men were put in charge of protecting a vast network of trenches that surrounded the Confederate capital. Work had begun on the fortifications surrounding the city in 1862, and two years later they were still being expanded. The first means of defense for the beleaguered capital was a ring of twenty-four star-shaped forts that surrounded the city. The forts themselves were small but very strong,

Lieutenant General Richard S. Ewell fell out of Lee's favor during the Overland Campaign and was given command of the Department of Richmond in June 1864. *Library of Congress.*

and they were manned by a force of heavy artillery units. Farther out from the star forts was the Intermediate Line, which extended in a five-mile radius from the state capital. This line was usually left undefended, as it was intended to serve as a reserve line in case of a serious emergency.

Even farther out was the Outer Defense Line, which had been built at the behest of Lee when he first took command of the Army of Northern Virginia in June 1862 (when he had been derisively called the "King of Spades"). This line ran for twenty-six miles from Chaffin's Bluff along the James out to the Chickahominy River east of the city. Even farther out from the Outer Line was the Exterior Line, designed to protect the city from an attack on the peninsula. This particular line ran from Chaffin's Bluff, cutting north past Nine Mile Road to the heights of the Chickahominy River.

In 1862, work also began on what would become known as the New Market Line—a line of defensive works constructed to protect the New Market Road, one of the key eastern approaches to Richmond. The New Market Line extended out from the Exterior Line and was still being improved when the Battle of New Market Heights took place. With such an extensive series of works surrounding Richmond, there was no possible way that Lee's army could man every square inch of the defenses. Lee and his compatriots knew this and "counted on occupying [the works] with mobile reserves…to meet specific threats. They were confident that the foe could no more attack the entire line simultaneously than they could defend it." Not everyone shared that confidence, however. Ewell's aide-de-camp recalled the dire situation north of the James:

> *This alarming state of affairs was pointed out by Gen. Ewell to Gen. Lee repeatedly—but as the need was equally great elsewhere, the Com'g. Gen'l. always informed him he could spare no troops & referred him to the Depts. at Richmond for assistance. Having failed everywhere else & meeting with no comfort from the Secr. of War, who took his representations quietly, he addressed in the latter part of Sept. a very urgent appeal to Gov. Smith & Mayor [Joseph] Mayo took the measure of sending down all the Federal prisoners who would volunteer to work (from the Libby). Some negroes were also collected & sent down & the Govr dispatched some convicts from the Penitentiary.*

The Confederates would have to rely on the soldiers in the trenches to avert disaster.[21]

The men who would defend these works against the Union onslaught on September 29, 1864, during the Battle of New Market Heights were a mixed group of veterans and low-quality city defense troops. Anchoring both ends of the New Market Line was artillery. Cannoneers of the 1st Rockbridge Artillery manned five guns out toward the far left of the Confederate line, while the right was defended by two guns manned by the 3rd Richmond Howitzers. In between these two artillery emplacements were rifle pits manned by infantry and dismounted cavalry. A portion of Brigadier General Martin W. Gary's dismounted cavalry supported the Rockbridge Artillery on the crest of New Market Heights, but most of his men were located farther south in the rifle pits themselves.

Lieutenant Colonel John C. Pemberton's name was made infamous after he lost Vicksburg (and his army) in 1863. In 1864, the distrusted Philadelphia Quaker was in charge of the artillery defenses around Richmond. *Library of Congress.*

Martin Witherspoon Gary of South Carolina was a Harvard graduate who entered Wade Hampton's famous legion as a captain. "The Bald Eagle," as he was sometimes known, commanded the Hampton Legion, the 7th South Carolina Cavalry and the 24th Virginia Cavalry.

To the horse soldiers' right, the line was defended by Lieutenant Colonel John Gregg's Texas Brigade. This was the celebrated unit that had formerly been commanded by John Bell Hood and that was often referred to, even after his departure, as "Hood's Texas Brigade." Alabama native John Gregg, "a rugged and unrelenting fighter" who was known to be fearless on the field of battle, had been a member of the Provisional Confederate Congress in 1861 before joining Hood's Texans. Gregg had been wounded at Chickamauga, and when he recovered, he was given the supreme honor of commanding the Texas Brigade. These fierce fighters had made their presence felt on battlefields stretching from Gaines's Mill, Gettysburg and the Wilderness in the east to Chickamauga in the western theater. Connecting with Gary's cavalrymen was the 1st Texas, which guarded a section of the line where a stream known as Four Mile Creek penetrated

Brigadier General John Gregg was a capable commander and led the Texas Brigade well during Butler's fall offensive north of the James River. He would be killed in action nine days after the Battle of New Market Heights. *Cook Collection, Valentine Richmond History Center.*

the Rebel lines and flowed southward. Next to the 1st were the 4th and 5th Texas, followed by the 3rd Arkansas (which, being the only Arkansas unit in the Army of Northern Virginia, was jokingly referred to as the "Third Texas" by Bass's men).[22]

Lieutenant Colonel Wyatt M. Elliott's 25th Virginia Battalion (also called the City Battalion) extended the line westward on the morning of the twenty-ninth. When the fighting broke out, Gregg stationed himself near Fort Harrison and left Colonel Frederick Samuel Bass in charge of the New Market Line. Bass was born in Virginia and had graduated from the Virginia Military Institute before joining the 1st Texas Infantry Regiment as a captain. Although his available force numbered fewer than 1,800 men, both the Texas Brigade and Gary's cavalry were first-rate soldiers who had proven themselves on the field of battle.

On September 29, 1864, they would meet soldiers who had much less fighting experience but everything in the world to fight for.

Chapter 2

"MR. BUTLER AND
HIS ETHIOPIAN COHORTS"

BEAST BUTLER, UNITED STATES COLORED TROOPS AND
THE ARMY OF THE JAMES

History has not been kind to the Civil War career of Ben Butler. A combination of awkward physique, a reputation for political conniving and rumors of military ineptitude dogged the general from the time he first lent his services to the Union cause in 1861. One historian later described him as "45, squat, obese, with a pudgy, ravaged face and one 'lop-eye,' he resembled a dissipated toad." While Butler certainly will not take his place beside the great heroes of the Union such as Grant, Sherman and Sheridan, one of his major contributions to Union victory came in the ways in which he utilized African Americans to support the war effort. Butler changed from a proslavery Democrat on the eve of the Civil War to a Radical Republican in command of the army that contained the largest percentage of United States Colored Troops—the nearly forgotten Army of the James.[23]

Benjamin Franklin Butler was born in Deerfield, New Hampshire, on November 5, 1818. His boyhood dream was to attend the United States Military Academy at West Point, but he was never able to obtain an appointment. Like many young men of his era who were unable to find success in the field in which they desired to work, Butler ended up studying law. After showing the tenacity that would make him legendary in the years to come, young Ben Butler established himself as one of the most flamboyant and provocative attorneys in the city of Lowell, Massachusetts. After his law practice began to flourish, Butler became more attuned to the political controversies of the day. While in Lowell, he also found an outlet for his martial passions in the form of the local militia company.[24]

Major General Benjamin F. "Beast" Butler was a lightning rod for controversy during the entire course of the Civil War. A supporter of using black troops in combat roles, Butler would make his United States Colored Troops the vanguard of his assault on the New Market Line. *Library of Congress.*

While Ben established himself and raised a family, he increasingly became involved in local and national politics. He gravitated toward the Democratic Party, and once he declared his loyalties to this party, the Whigs of Lowell began to feel his sting (he once vowed during a political controversy that if he didn't get his way he would reduce the city to "a sheep pasture and a fishing place"). By the time of the presidential election of 1860, Butler was a Democratic powerhouse and had risen to the rank of brigadier general in the state militia of Massachusetts. However, the critical issues that had divided the nation conspired to divide the Democrats as well, and Butler found himself in the unique position of nominating none other than Jefferson Davis—future president of the Confederate States of America—more than fifty times for the ticket. He failed in this measure, and when the party split into Northern and Southern wings, Butler supported Southern candidate John C. Breckinridge (former vice president of the United States and future Confederate secretary of war). Thus, when Abraham Lincoln was announced as the victor of the presidential contest, Butler found himself standing on the wrong side of history, and he worked quickly to restore his reputation.[25]

Having erred in the arena of politics, Butler relied on his association with the state militia to prove his fealty to the Union once the Civil War was underway. He was able to convince newly elected governor John A. Andrew to appoint him the commanding general of all Massachusetts troops who were about to take the field. As events would show, his was a crooked road to embracing emancipation and the use of blacks as soldiers. His first misstep came when he was marching his soldiers to Baltimore in April 1861. On April 19, the soldiers of the 6th Massachusetts had been fired upon by an angry secessionist mob, and Butler wanted to avoid another such scene at all costs. He therefore wrote to Governor Thomas H. Hicks and asked permission for his men to pass through his state on their way to the nation's capital. To set the governor at ease, Butler offered his soldiers to the governor should there be an uprising of the state's slaves—something most Marylanders were concerned about during the turbulent opening period of the war. A few months after this seemingly proslavery gesture, the general found himself at Fort Monroe on the Virginia peninsula.[26]

In May, Butler found that his command was flooded with slaves seeking refuge within his lines. The reason that there were so many slaves nearby was because Confederate forces were using them to construct fortifications of their own. From the outset of the war, the Confederacy had been quick to utilize its slave population to free up most of the available white men to serve in the army and navy. When some angry slave owners showed up to reclaim their "property"—something they could legally do under the Fugitive Slave Act of 1850—Butler reversed the stance he had taken in Maryland and refused to let the slaves return to their masters. In a loyal state like Maryland, Butler would be required by federal law to return the runaways, but since Virginia had seceded and declared itself to be part of a nation other than the United States, Butler cleverly turned this against the owners by declaring these slaves to be "contraband of war" and therefore liable to seizure under international law. The term "contraband" caught on and quickly became the standard descriptor for runaway slaves who had made their way over into Union lines. The *National Intelligencer* purported that Butler's contraband policy was the way every commander should handle similar situations and stated that "it is just as clearly right to transfer these slaves as fast as possible from the corn fields to the trenches as it is to appropriate a drove of the enemy's beeves from his to our own shambles."[27]

In July 1862, when Butler had moved on to command the Department of the Gulf, the political general backslid again when he denied General John W. Phelps's attempt to recruit black soldiers in Louisiana. Phelps was an abolitionist from Vermont who was determined to inculcate his political principles with his military responsibilities, and this soon made him run afoul of Butler. Phelps, as it turned out, had armed fugitive slaves under his own authority in an effort to raise three regiments of black troops. Butler ordered Phelps to desist with his scheme and instead have these contrabands set to work building fortifications. Phelps, his sensibilities grievously wounded, declared to Butler, "I am not willing to become the mere slave driver which you propose" and resigned. Much drama ensued as Butler scolded Phelps and refused to accept his resignation. By August, Phelps was finally able to resign, and Butler, who had now become convinced of the soundness of Phelps's plan, "claimed credit for initiating black enlistment" in Louisiana. The men Butler enlisted were part of the famous Louisiana Native Guard, and it would seem that old Ben Butler would finally stay on the side of black enlistment for the remainder of the war. Indeed, in October 1863, Butler returned to Fort Monroe to organize what would become the Army of the James. It is thought that he was planning on using his military successes to insert himself back into the political arena—and just in time for the presidential election of 1864, no less. Still, in his tenure as army commander, Butler would prove once and for all that he was off the fence when it came to supporting African Americans as soldiers.[28]

Much like its prominent commander, the Army of the James has come down as a fascinating yet flawed caricature in much of the literature pertaining to the Civil War. For more than 130 years, it languished without a major study written about it, and when that day came, the work's title described it as an *Army of Amateurs*. While it is certainly true that the Army of the James contained more former politicians and so-called political generals than it did West Point graduates, the army certainly was not lacking when it came to hard-fighting officers and enlisted men. As Alfred Terry said to a gathering of fellow high-ranking officers shortly after the war, "Whatever of reputation all, or any of us, may have acquired…is due, not so much to our own merit, as to the merit of those we commanded, the subordinate officers and the private soldiers of the Army of the James." The army was split into two corps. By September 1864, the 10th Corps was under the command of Major General David B. Birney, a veteran of the Army of the Potomac whose father was a famous abolitionist. The 18th Corps was under the command of Major General Edward O.C. Ord, who had been described as a "bluff, irascible, impetuous, willful old regular." Indeed, this small fighting force that numbered no more than thirty-six thousand men throughout the course of the war was unique in many aspects.[29]

With Butler at the helm to satisfy his curiosity when it came to new technologies that were just beginning to emerge during the Civil War, the

Army of the James found itself on the cutting edge in several areas. First of all, Butler had excellent signalmen working with him to ensure that information on enemy troop movements was gathered and disseminated quickly—a trait that would come in handy at New Market Heights. Butler even went so far as to meddle with Greek fire (unsuccessfully), experiment with armor-piercing rounds that he hoped could blast through the plating of Confederate ironclads and encourage the development of small, portable cameras that could be used in signal towers and observation balloons. The Army of the James also invested in the newfangled Gatling gun, which at the time was perfect for guarding bridges. When it came to caring for sick and wounded soldiers, the Army of the James again excelled, although it may or may not have had something to do with the fact that Clara Barton was in charge of 10th Corps hospitals in 1864. All in all, the leadership of the Army of the James was not afraid to step outside conventional wisdom when it came to new innovations. However, perhaps the army's most radical innovation was the way in which it employed African American soldiers.[30]

Ever since the opening shots at Fort Sumter in April 1861, African Americans had been clamoring to get into the fight. While early forms of black recruitment such as those initiated by Phelps failed, pressure was put on the Lincoln administration to let free blacks and slaves fight for their citizenship and freedom, respectively. One of the most persistent and eloquent spokesmen for black enlistment was Frederick Douglass. He knew that African Americans serving in blue would have to fight a "double battle against slavery at the South and against prejudice…at the North." Still, Douglass posited that "going into the army is the speediest way to overcome the prejudice that has dictated unjust laws against us." Douglass went on to say that "once in the United States uniform and the colored man has a springing board under him by which he can jump to loftier heights."[31]

The long road to black participation in the Union war effort began in 1862, was made a government policy by the Emancipation Proclamation as of January 1, 1863, and crystallized with the establishment of the Bureau of Colored Troops by the United States War Department on May 22, 1863, under General Orders No. 143. This order stipulated that the Bureau of Colored Troops was designed "for the record of all matters relating to the organization of Colored Troops." The units established by the bureau would be commanded by white officers and made up of black enlisted men. Any white man, enlisted or officer, who wished to command colored troops must first go through a process of examination by boards that "will be convened at such posts as may be decided upon by the War Department to examine applicants for commissions to command colored troops, who, on Application to the Adjutant General, may receive authority to present themselves to the board for examination." Furthermore, "all non-commissioned officers may be selected and appointed from the best men of their number in the usual mode of appointing non-commissioned officers."[32]

By May 1864, the Army of the James consisted of thirty-five thousand soldiers, of which about eight thousand were United States Colored Troops. While many officers deemed having USCT units in their brigades and divisions as a blemish on their fighting prowess, Butler by this point had grown to believe in his black soldiers and scorned the "stupid, unreasoning, and quite vengeful prejudice against them among the regular officers of our army." It appears that the USCTs in the Army of the James reciprocated those feelings. One incident witnessed by war correspondent Charles A. Page of the *New York Tribune* illustrates the loyalty felt by many black soldiers toward Butler. A rumor had spread throughout camp that Butler had been replaced as commander of the Army of the James. According to Page:

[A squad of black soldiers] *presented themselves at the office of Lieutenant Brown, then mustering officer here, and demanded to be mustered out. They had heard that General Butler's "time was out," they had enlisted to fight under him and they "wasn't goin' t' hab any udder man generalizin' fer dem," and they were quieted only by the assurance that General Butler's time was not out.*[33]

For the black troops who would storm New Market Heights, the men who would lead them into battle were an interesting menagerie of New England Yankees who all despised the institution of slavery. The division that would do all of the heavy fighting at New Market Heights was the 3rd Division of the 18th Corps, commanded by Brigadier General Charles Paine. This division was distinctive in that it was entirely made up of United States Colored Troops units.

Thirty-one-year-old Charles Jackson Paine was born in Boston to a prominent family and graduated from Harvard in 1853. Paine then became an attorney, and when war broke out, he became a captain in the 22nd Massachusetts Infantry. In 1862, he served under Butler and worked his way up to becoming a member of Butler's staff in March 1864. Being under Butler's care turned out to be prosperous for the young officer, and on July 4, 1864, he was appointed a brigadier general and took command of the 3rd Division of the 18th Corps one month later. Fondly known as "Jack," the young officer had a good rapport with his men; after his promotion was announced, he wrote that "one of my darkies chalked up on our cook

Shown later in life, Brigadier General Charles J. Paine's inexperience at handling his division in combat would lead to heavy losses at New Market Heights. *Testimonial to Charles J. Paine.*

house, 'Jack is a Brigadier General. Jack has been much more important since.'" When he took over his new command, he took to reading Richmond newspapers every day to see how his enemies were viewing the war. When it came to being a field commander, however, Paine was "mediocre and relatively inexperienced." At New Market Heights, Paine's men would learn firsthand what that inexperience would cost them.[34]

Paine's 1st Brigade was under the command of Colonel John H. Holman. A native of Maine, Holman was thirty-nine at the time of New Market Heights. He was an architect before the war and was residing in Missouri when the Civil War began. He was commissioned a second lieutenant in the Missouri Reserve Corps and eventually rose to command of the 1st USCT. Described as "a taciturn soldier and Unionist," Holman viewed slavery as a "curse" and tried his hand at songwriting when he wrote the rally song for the 1st USCT. One stanza that displayed his zeal went:

> *Hi rally! Ho rally! To the war we'll go*
> *And we'll show those traitors south the courage of their foe!*
> *Come what may—now's the day*
> *The year of jubilee!*
> *Dawn is nigh with freedom's ray*
> *Mankind must now be free!*

Colonel John Holman was known as a strong Union man with antislavery views. In 1864, he commanded the First Brigade of Paine's Division—a unit that would see limited combat at New Market Heights. *Library of Congress.*

By September 1864, Holman commanded a brigade composed of the 1st, 22nd and 37th USCT.[35]

The 1st USCT was a unit that was recruited in Washington, D.C., in May 1863. It was trained at Camp Green on the Potomac River by Colonel William Birney. It was such a prominent unit that many notable visitors went to watch the black soldiers train. One prominent visitor was Walt Whitman, who recorded going to Georgetown, "where the niggers have their first Washington regiment encamped," and wryly noted that "since they have begun to carry arms, the Secesh here…are not as insulting to them as formerly." The unit saw its first large-scale fighting at Baylor's Farm at Petersburg on June 15, 1864, and was sent to work on the Dutch Gap Canal before New Market Heights. The 22nd USCT was organized at Camp William Penn, Philadelphia, during January 1864 and also saw heavy fighting at Baylor's Farm, where it "headed the charge…and captured six of the seven guns taken by the division, and two of the four forts." It was also assigned to the Dutch Gap Canal by August 1864. The third regiment under Holman's command was the 37th USCT. Originally the 3rd North Carolina

"Mr. Butler and His Ethiopian Cohorts"

The 1st United States Colored Infantry on parade. This unit was organized around Washington, D.C., and would fight under Holman's command in 1864. *Library of Congress.*

An image of Company E, 4th USCT, at Fort Lincoln in Washington, D.C., taken on November 17, 1865. While the new uniforms and equipment might lead one to believe that these were brand-new soldiers, the odds are that this remnant of Company E saw hard-fought service at New Market Heights and elsewhere. *Library of Congress.*

Colored Volunteers, this unit was made up of recruits mainly from North Carolina and Virginia. Bad fortune seemed to follow this unit wherever it went. Even though it was organized over the winter of 1863–64, some recruits still did not know how to load their muskets as of March. Also, since the unit saw very little action before New Market Heights, it had a high desertion rate.[36]

Commanding the 2nd Brigade of Paine's Division was Colonel Alonzo Granville Draper. Born in Brattleboro, Vermont, Draper was twenty-nine years old at the time of New Market Heights. A serious boy from the very start, Draper's parents said that he was a "lawyer in embryo" before he turned eight years old. By 1860, Draper had become an advocate for industrial workers and had led the "Shoemaker's Strike" in Lynn, Massachusetts. Young Draper was studying for the bar in Lynn when the Civil War erupted and was elected the captain of Company C, 1st Massachusetts Heavy Artillery. In August 1863, he became the colonel of the 2nd North Carolina Infantry, which was later redesignated the 36th USCT. Draper had stated that he had a "sincere desire to assist in ameliorating the condition of the colored race and in their enfranchisement from that social depression to which an ignorant popular prejudice has consigned them." However, Draper did not give everyone the impression that he would be a natural leader in command of

Colonel Alonzo G. Draper was known as a dour person and a "severe disciplinarian." In spite of this, he led his men with courage and skill in his assault on the New Market Line. *From* The Drapers in America.

colored troops. When asked about Draper's fitness for command of colored troops, Colonel Thomas B. Tannatt said that "he thought him a too severe disciplinarian for that race." Only time would tell if Tannatt's prediction of Draper had any truth in it.[37]

The 5th USCT began forming at Camp Delaware, Ohio, in June 1863 and was originally known as the 127th Ohio Volunteer Infantry (Colored). One of the enlisted men who helped raise recruits was Milton M. Holland, who would go on to receive the Medal of Honor for his actions at New Market Heights. Addressing a crowd of prospective recruits, Holland told them that "there is a bright day coming for the colored man, and he must sacrifice home comforts, and his blood if necessary, to speed the coming of that glorious day." After a period of training, the regiment was ready for service by September 1863. The unit was given a regimental flag inscribed with the motto "Victory or Death" and was sent to the front. The 5th participated in raids in North Carolina in late 1863 and had a minor role in the Kilpatrick-Dahlgren Raid in February and March 1864. The unit was then sent to the Petersburg front, where it stayed until late August, when it was sent to Deep Bottom on the James River. The 36th USCT was birthed from the 2nd North Carolina Colored Volunteers, which was raised in New Bern, North Carolina. The rank and file of the 36th consisted mainly of former slaves from Virginia and North Carolina, and the unit was ready to be deployed by October 1863. After the 36th was assigned to guard Confederate prisoners at Point Lookout Prison in Maryland, it was involved in several controversial shootings while facing harassment from white Federal soldiers also stationed there. After departing Point Lookout, the 36th raided along the Rappahannock River, led by Draper, and was then sent to Petersburg. The 38th USCT was organized in Virginia in early 1864 and stayed on duty at Norfolk and Portsmouth until June 1864, when it was sent to the Richmond-Petersburg front.[38]

Rounding out Paine's Division was Colonel Samuel A. Duncan's 3rd Brigade, which by the time of New Market Heights would only consist of the 4th and 6th USCT. Born in Plainfield, New Hampshire, Duncan was only twenty-eight years old when he led his fateful initial assault against the New Market Line. Duncan graduated from Dartmouth College in 1858 and became a major in the 14th New Hampshire in September 1862. Stating that it was "much to a man's credit and honor to lead a black regt.," Duncan applied to become an officer with the Bureau of Colored Troops and "passed for colonel in class 1, ranking first out of about two hundred examinations." Described as "a man of intellect, breeding, and military acumen, with an

Colonel Samuel A. Duncan eagerly volunteered to lead black soldiers in 1863 and passed his examinations with some of the highest scores on record. His zeal and intelligence served him well when he led his men into the maelstrom of New Market Heights. *Companions of MOLLUS.*

active social conscience and a desire to make African-Americans an effective tool in the struggle to restore the Union," Duncan earned the respect of his men and rose to brigade command through unquestionable merit and skill.[39]

The 4th USCT was organized in Baltimore, Maryland, during the summer of 1863—a time when Maryland was still a slave state that was loyal to the Union. This made recruiting a tricky business, but the regiment moved to Fort Monroe on October 1, 1863, and then to Yorktown. The regiment had the misfortune of participating in two failed cavalry raids: Wistar's raid against Richmond in February 1864 and the Kilpatrick-Dahlgren Raid of late February and early March. In May, the unit joined the rest of the Army of the James in its movement to Bermuda Hundred, where it saw sharp fighting at Spring Hill on May 18, 1864. The 4th was also present for the fighting at Baylor's Farm at Petersburg and had a supporting role in the disastrous Battle of the Crater fought on July 30, 1864. Before New Market Heights, the unit was set to work on the Dutch Gap Canal. The 6th USCT was organized at Camp William Penn from July to September 1863. Its first duty was at Yorktown, where it stayed until it was sent on General Edward A. Wild's expedition to North Carolina in December 1863. The unit also went with the 4th USCT in its adventures with the Federal cavalry in February and March 1864. In May 1864, the 6th helped capture City Point near Petersburg and was also at Baylor's Farm. It would also pay its dues digging the Dutch Gap Canal. Duncan also was given the 10th USCT and about one hundred raw recruits, who arrived just before the September offensive against Richmond got underway. It was determined that those with little or no training could still work on the Dutch Gap Canal, while the 4th and 6th USCT would go off and fight on their own.[40]

Also accompanying Paine's men in this foray against the New Market Line was Brigadier General William Birney's Colored Brigade of the 10th Corps. Birney was the older brother of the corps commander and had been instrumental in recruiting and organizing many of the USCT units that were about to go into battle. Under his command were the 29th Connecticut (Colored), 7th USCT, 8th USCT, 9th USCT and the 45th USCT. The 2nd United States Colored Cavalry was also placed under Paine's command and would fight as dismounted skirmishers when the battle broke out.

In an interesting historical footnote, the black soldiers who would go into combat at New Market Heights were not the only minorities serving in their respective regiments. As one historian noted, "Twenty-five German speaking officers served in the thirteen participating USCT regiments at that time, the highest number of ethnic officers in any campaign during the war."[41]

While there were innumerable differences between Benjamin Butler and the black troops under his command, they had one very stark reality in common: if they were captured on the field of battle, they would not be subject to the normal rules of warfare. Whereas in most Civil War battles, any man who put down his weapon and surrendered was taken prisoner and either sent to a POW camp or paroled, the Confederacy held both "Beast" Butler and the African American soldiers in his army in contempt. For Butler, an executive order had been issued by Confederate president Jefferson Davis that was still standing. Due to Butler's allegedly harsh treatment of Confederate civilians in New Orleans, Davis claimed that Butler and all officers serving under him were "declared not entitled to be considered as soldiers engaged in honorable warfare, but as robbers and criminals, deserving death; and that they and each of them be, whenever captured, reserved for execution." The order went on to state that "all negro slaves captured in arms be at once delivered over to the executive authorities of the respective States to which they belong, to be dealt with according to the laws of said States." While this provision was aimed at the men of the Louisiana Native Guard and other black units that had fought under Butler in 1862, Davis made sure to also include the final proviso that "like orders be executed in all cases with respect to all commissioned officers of the United States when found serving in company with armed slaves in insurrection against the authorities of the different States of this Confederacy." In short, Ben Butler was a marked man.[42]

So, too, were the black men found under his, or any other Union officer's, command. Confederate secretary of war James A. Seddon had declared that "slaves in flagrant rebellion are subject to death by the laws of every slave-holding State…They cannot be recognized in any way as soldiers subject to the rules of war and to trial by military courts…summary execution must therefore be inflicted on those taken." While this policy proved nearly impossible for the Confederate War Department to uniformly enforce, there were plenty of instances when black Union soldiers were gunned down in cold blood in the act of trying to surrender. At places like Milliken's Bend and Olustee, chilling accounts of Confederate soldiers systematically executing any black survivors made it clear that Seddon's words were not idle talk. However, it was the alleged "massacre" at a place called Fort Pillow in Tennessee that caused the most furor and would give Butler's men their battle cry when they charged the works at New Market Heights.[43]

Fort Pillow was a bastion on the Mississippi River that contained a garrison of African American soldiers and what were known at the time as "Tennessee Tories"—natives of Tennessee who had volunteered to fight for the Union or, even worse, former Confederates who had switched sides when it looked like the North might prevail. When Confederate general Nathan Bedford Forrest's troopers stormed the fort, many black soldiers who were in the act of trying to surrender were shot down in cold blood. Bloodcurdling stories of atrocity swept through the Northern newspapers, and word trickled down quickly to the black units in all Union armies. The message was clear: if a black soldier was found wearing the uniform of the United States, he could expect to either be sent back into slavery or killed outright. Southern fears of slave insurrections were coming true, and the USCTs were the embodiment of those fears.

The Confederacy could not equivocate on such issues. Every man who went into battle at New Market Heights knew full well what could happen if he fell into Rebel hands. "Mr. Butler and his Ethiopian cohorts," as one Confederate soldier described them, were about to experience for themselves how wedded the defenders of Richmond were to their "peculiar" military doctrine.[44]

Chapter 3

"A LONG AND TEDIOUS TRAMP"

THE MARCH UP

The situation on the north side of the James River in mid-September 1864 had changed very little since the Richmond-Petersburg Campaign had kicked off in June. During that month, Grant had established a small bridgehead and fort that was built by the 10th Corps at a place called Deep Bottom, across the river from Jones Neck, in Henrico County. This bridgehead served as a springboard from which attacks could be launched in support of the Army of the Potomac's forays against Petersburg. The first time that large bodies of troops were used at Deep Bottom was on July 27, 1864, when Major General Winfield Scott Hancock's 2nd Corps of the Army of the Potomac, supported by two divisions of Phil Sheridan's cavalry, crossed over to the north side. Their goal was to compel Lee to send reinforcements away from the area where Major General Ambrose E. Burnside was set to explode the mine that his men had been preparing since late June. Lee was only too willing to oblige, and heavy fighting ensued along the Darbytown and New Market Roads. After two days of hard fighting, Hancock withdrew his men and returned to Petersburg only hours before the Battle of the Crater began.[45]

In mid-August, Hancock's beleaguered corps returned to Deep Bottom in an attack that preceded Grant's strike against the Weldon Railroad in Petersburg. This time, elements of Birney's 10th Corps would participate in the diversion. Once again, Hancock's men advanced up the New Market and Darbytown Roads against Rebel soldiers entrenched at Bailey's Creek and Fussell's Mill, near New Market Heights. While the fighting raged on August 16, the Federals received a stroke of luck when Confederate cavalry commander Brigadier General John R. Chambliss was killed. When Union soldiers came across his body, they immediately began hunting for souvenirs. In the process of cutting off uniform buttons and rummaging through his personal effects, they found a "most excellent map of Richmond and its defenses."

Four days later, Hancock's men withdrew yet again; since Grant had gained a foothold on the Weldon Railroad, there was no longer any need for their presence on the north side of the James. While it did not seem to accomplish much, the Second Battle of Deep Bottom, or Fussell's Mill as it was sometimes called, yielded an important piece of military intelligence. When Major Nathaniel Michler, chief engineer of the Army of the Potomac, received a copy of the map recovered from Chambliss's body, he had the map photographed and distributed seventeen copies, one of which landed in the lap of Ben Butler. It would prove to be an invaluable tool when he planned his September offensive.[46]

In late September, Grant prepared yet another attack on Petersburg that would require a third attack on the north side of the James. He planned an offensive in which the Army of the Potomac would launch an assault from its newly won lines on the Weldon Railroad and strike at the Boydton Plank Road and the Southside Railroad, which were two of Lee's remaining supply lines. Butler and his Army of the James would compose the strike force that would threaten Richmond. Luckily for Grant, Butler had been planning an attack against Richmond for quite some time. His spy network was busy compiling information on Confederate troop numbers. Using his copy of the map recovered from Chambliss's body, Butler later said that he "instructed my secret service men to find out exactly how many men were holding each fortification, including the works at Chaffin's farm and Fort Harrison, and the connecting lines of forts between them." These efforts were aided by Confederate deserters who frequently escaped to the bastion at Deep Bottom. W.S. Neel of the 15th Georgia later griped:

> The enemy by some means found out how weak our line was. I heard the day before we were attacked by two corps that a captain in charge of the picket line, I believe he belonged to the 15th Georgia, had deserted and gone over to the enemy giving away our whole situation. I can't vouch for this fact, but it was currently reported about camp the day before they attacked.

It took some time for Butler's scouts to gather the information that he needed, but according to his reminiscences, "about the 20th of September I went to General Grant and explained to him my preparation, and asked his leave to make an attack in that quarter."[47]

Six days after Butler met with Grant the first time, the two commanders made a reconnaissance by boat up the James to see the Confederate defenses firsthand. The two apparently agreed on the general outline for how the attack would take place. At some point, Butler made it plain to Grant that he wanted his black troops to spearhead this assault. Butler had been deeply disturbed by the recent Battle of the Crater and thought that the USCTs had been poorly led and thus had received an unfair portion of the blame for the defeat. Butler looked at Grant and said, "I want to convince myself whether, when under my own eye, the negro troops will fight; and if I can take with the negroes, a redoubt that turned Hancock's corps on a former occasion, that will settle the question." That same day, Butler wrote to his wife to say that "we are about to make a move, say the last of this week, which will be a very conclusive one if successful." Never one to miss an opportunity to jest, Butler played on the term that he had made famous three years earlier and said, "I must not write more about it as it is 'contraband.'"[48]

On September 27, the pace of events quickened, and Grant wired Butler from City Point with detailed instructions based on their conversation the night before. Grant stated that Butler must "prepare [his] Army according to the verbal instructions already given for moving on the morning of the 29th inst." Not one to leave any doubts about how the operation was to be conducted, Grant told Butler that "the movement should be commenced at night" and that the primary objective of the operation was "to surprise and capture Richmond if possible." If taking the Rebel capital was not possible, the secondary objective of Butler's movement was to tie up enough of Lee's men to allow the Army of the Potomac's efforts against Petersburg to succeed. Grant wanted Butler's men to travel light, ordering that "they will take only a single blanket rolled and carried over the shoulder, three days rations in haversacks, and sixty rounds of ammunition…No wagons will be taken." Grant concluded his instructions by reemphasizing to Butler that "if the enemy resists you by sufficient force to prevent your advance, it is confidently expected that Gen. Meade can gain a decisive advantage… The prize sought is either Richmond or Petersburg, or a position which will secure the fall of the latter." When he received Grant's telegram, Butler sprang into action and wired back, "[T]he dispositions are being made."[49]

The dispositions that Butler made produced a sixteen-page battle order that was chock-full of minute details and left very little to chance. On the evening of September 28, the army commander summoned his three subordinates—Major General David B. Birney, Major General Edward O.C. Ord and Brigadier General August V. Kautz—to his headquarters at Point of Rocks to explain the parts that they would play in the upcoming assault. Relying on the strategic abilities that he had been honing since he first took field command and the intelligence supplied by his spy network, he gave his executive officers the detailed orders that they would need to capture the Rebel capital. The object of the mission, he stated, was

> [t]o surprise the Confederate forces in our front here, and, passing them, to get possession of the city of Richmond. Failing that, to make such serious and determined demonstration to that end as shall draw re-enforcements from the right of the enemy's line in sufficient numbers so as to enable the Army of the Potomac to move upon the enemy's communication near Petersburg.[50]

Butler was able to supply comprehensive details about the locations of Confederate troops and the strength of each unit, and his knowledge of the troops holding the New Market Line was truly impressive. He was able to estimate that

> [t]he Twenty-fifth Virginia (City Battalion), numbering not to exceed 200 men for duty, are extended along the line toward Ruffin's house, in front of our position at Deep Bottom. They are there joined by Benning's old (Georgia) brigade, commanded by Colonel Du Bose, numbering about 400 men, who are extended along the line past Ruffin's house, the picket-line being near the house of J. Aiken. They are there joined by Gregg's (Texas) brigade, numbering about 400 men for duty, who extend along the line to a place called New Market, where the enemy have a pretty strong work on a height commanding the New Market road. These are all the infantry forces, except a battalion of militia reserves, numbering about 175 men for duty, who are in camp some distance to the rear, who form a connecting line between Johnson's brigade and the City Battalion. These reserves are composed of soldiers below the age of eighteen and above the age of forty-five; but they, with the City Battalion, have never been under fire. At the place marked on the map "Drill-Room" is stationed a regiment believed to be about 400 men, the Seventh South Carolina Cavalry. At the place marked "Sweeney's Pottery" Wade Hampton's Legion, numbering about 400 men, are stationed on the easterly side of Four-Mile Creek and Bailey's Run, apparently to guard the road by which General Hancock

advanced over Strawberry Plains from below Four-Mile Creek, and picketing toward Malvern Hill. In the rear, at the intersection of the roads near the point marked "W. Throgmorton" is a regiment, the Twenty-fourth Virginia Cavalry, numbering about 400 men. On Chaffin's farm there is no garrison, except about 100 heavy artillerists, holding that place as an intrenched camp.[51]

Butler stressed that his men would have a further advantage in that the Confederates could only be reinforced by troops crossing the pontoon bridges on the James at Chaffin's Bluff. The plan next detailed the specifics of the plan of attack. Butler's troops were to cross the James and advance in two columns. Major General Edward Ord, with two 18th Corps divisions, was to cross the river at a place called Aiken's Landing and then turn west, back toward the river, and seize the Confederate bridges at and above Chaffin's Bluff. After this was accomplished, Ord's men were to push up the Osborne Turnpike, which ran straight into the eastern approaches to Richmond. Meanwhile, Birney's 10th Corps would cross at Jones Neck, advance through the Deep Bottom bridgehead and storm the Confederate lines guarding the New Market Road. Birney would then wheel left and follow the New Market and Darbytown Roads to Richmond, roughly paralleling Ord's advance. The final element of the plan called for the inept cavalry commander August V. Kautz to also cross at Jones Neck and push out of Deep Bottom, riding hard and fast to the Darbytown Road, where they would race for Richmond. If all worked according to plan, Butler would have two prongs of infantry and one of cavalry—totaling twenty-six thousand men—rolling inexorably on the hapless Rebel capital. Butler concluded by emphasizing:

The commanding general cannot refrain in closing these instructions from pressing one or two points upon the attention of corps commanders: First, the necessity of being ready to move and moving at the moment designated; second, the fact that the commanding general is under no substantial mistake in regard to the force to be at first encountered, and therefore there is no necessity of time spent in reconnoitering or taking special care of the flanks of the moving columns. The commanding general would also recommend to the corps commanders, as soon as it may be done with safety from discovering the movement, to impress upon each of the division commanders, with directions for them to transmit the information through their subordinates even to the privates, of the number and kind of troops we are required to meet, so there may be no panic from supposed flanking movements of the

The pontoon bridge at Deep Bottom. *National Archives.*

enemy or attacks in the rear, always a source of demoralization when the troops do not understand the force of the enemy. Let us assure and instruct our men that we are able to fight anything we will find either in front or flank or rear, wherever they may happen to be.

Finally, Butler told his subordinates that every man in the first unit to set foot in Richmond would receive a promotion to the next higher grade and six months' extra pay. After ensuring that each officer knew his job thoroughly, Butler concluded the meeting.[52]

About this time, a British correspondent from *Fraser's Magazine for Town and Country* arrived at Butler's headquarters. The correspondent stated that "General Butler's welcome was most courteous and kind. Though he was engaged with General Birney…making final arrangements for his advance the next morning, he conversed for some minutes on general subjects." After Birney had departed to put his part of the plan into action, Butler told this foreign journalist that "he was going to advance upon Richmond the next morning." Butler even "produced a copy by photography of the map of the environs of Richmond [the Chambliss map] and pointed out the routes by which his army was to advance the next morning." After the correspondent had retired for the evening, Butler wrote to his wife: "I shall be very busy now for a day or two, and perhaps not in connection with the mails, so that you need not think it strange if you do not get a letter for a day or two." The contemplative general closed his missive, imploring his wife, "Kiss me, dearest, and believe me."[53]

When the time came to mobilize, Paine's Division was fortunate enough to have the luxury of piling into gunboats and transport ships to take the men from Dutch Gap upriver to Deep Bottom. Captain McMurray remembered that the 6th USCT "was on a steamer, ready to proceed...We started about dark, and before midnight were put on shore at Deep Bottom, where we rested without shelter of any kind until morning." Sergeant Major Christian Fleetwood of the 4th USCT wrote in his diary that evening that "after much tribulation and several unsuccessful attempts to catch a nap, we embarked on board a gunboat and debarked at Jones Landing. Marched up to works. Bivouacked at Deep Bottom." Thus, the three brigade commanders under Paine had mustered and assembled their respective units, and the 3rd Division was poised to spearhead the advance from Deep Bottom. However, all was not well with their comrades in the 10th Corps.[54]

Due to the ultrasecret environment in which Butler had explained the plan of attack to his subordinates, David Birney—by all accounts a good and punctual soldier—did not move his troops out on the afternoon of Tuesday, September 27, as Butler had planned. Instead, Birney's men broke camp at 3:00 p.m. on the afternoon of Wednesday, September 28. The 1st Division led the way, with the 2nd Division following close behind, and as the column began to cross the Appomattox River at Broadway Landing, everything appeared to be going as planned. However, this did not bode well for the upcoming attack.

The 10th Corps was the main striking force for the right wing of Butler's two-pronged assault north of the James. It was the 10th Corps, supplemented by Paine's Division of the 18th Corps, that would strike the New Market Line at 4:00 a.m. on the morning of the twenty-ninth. If they were late arriving on the field of battle, that could throw Butler's intricate timetables off-kilter, and the element of surprise deemed so vital by the army commander might be lost.

It appears as if Birney misunderstood Butler's intentions and thought that he was to move his corps preparatory to a movement by water to another front altogether. Butler intended for this to be a ruse to fool the Confederates as to the true destination of the 10th Corps, but the ruse worked so well that even Birney thought it to be the truth. Since he thought that this march was only one part of a bigger logistical maneuver, Birney did not provide the marching orders that would usually accompany a corps that was on its way to the jumping-off point for a major attack. By the time Birney had learned what his men were truly expected to do at the Point of Rocks conference on the evening of Wednesday the twenty-eighth, his men had been on the march for several hours. One of Birney's early biographers wrote in 1867:

> From the nature of the orders given, the staff and general officers of the corps were, of course, aware that a movement was contemplated, but to what point or for what purpose they could not divine. At the time of its commencement there were a number of transports collected at City Point, and rumor said that the Tenth Corps was destined for Wilmington, N.C. This impression was confirmed by the fact that General [Charles K.] Graham, who commanded the army flotilla, composing part of the Army of the James, had just returned from a reconnaissance near Wilmington.[55]

While their commander was busy learning the true nature of what was to transpire in a few hours, some of his men also began to speculate that they were on their way to board troop transports that would take them away from the stagnant trench warfare that they had grown to despise during their tenure at Petersburg. As one soldier recalled:

> Many were the conjectures as to what might be the nature of this change. Most thought we were to take transports, and to what point none knew. All, however, were anxious to get away from the vicinity of the Army of the Potomac, which seemed destined to receive the hardest blows and least glory, in the war.[56]

When the men reached Bermuda Hundred, they thought that they had reached their final destination. However, as the sun began to set, they were ordered to keep going—it turned out that they still had another eight miles to go before bedding down for the night. As darkness fell, what promised to be a quick march from Petersburg to Deep Bottom turned into an arduous and painstaking ordeal. The pace of the march slowed down, and confusion reigned supreme. The column sputtered ahead in fits and starts, and this began to take a physical and mental toll on the men.

As the temperature began to drop and stars began to appear in the evening sky, the most frustrating obstacle in the way of the marchers was the wagon train of the 1st Division. These large wagons, brimming with ammunition that was sure to be expended the next day, could pose difficulties during the day, but during an evening march they proved to be a major hindrance to Birney's troops. The chaplain of the 112th New York later griped that the march "would have been easier had the 1st Division been moved in proper season, so that its train need not obstruct the movement of the 2nd." The 2nd Division's commander, Brigadier General Robert S. Foster, later explained

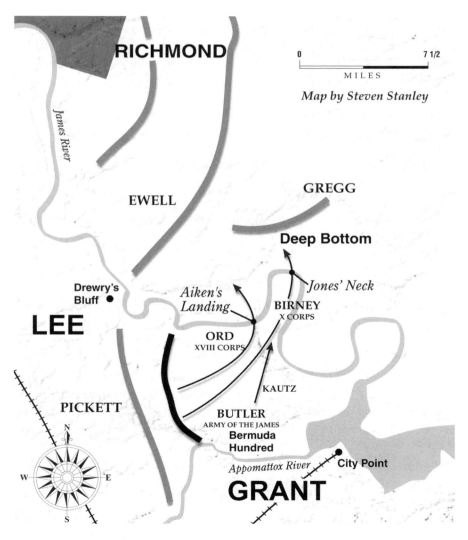

Butler consolidates his forces on the evening of September 28. *Steven Stanley, cartographer.*

that "owing to delays in the wagon train of [the 1st] division my progress was slow, and the head of my column only reached the pontoon bridge across the Appomattox at 8:35 p.m."[57] It was going to be a long night.

A soldier in the 11th Maine looked back on the trying advance of the 10th Corps and stated that "night marches are always wearying ones. The monotony of plodding through silent darkness, hour after hour, is as wearying to the men as is the distance. It is rarely that a gleam of enjoyment illumines the dullness of such a march." Another soldier grumbled of "one of those forced night marches which scatter a regiment and brigade, mixing front and rear for miles." Moving along narrow country lanes with men marching four abreast, wagons lumbering ahead and staff officers and orderlies flitting up and down the sides of the roads produced congestion, and the column would have to stop periodically to untangle itself or make sure that it was not heading in the wrong direction.[58]

As the night dragged on, more and more men began to straggle and fall out by the side of the road. As one historian noted, "The X Corps virtually fell to pieces as it moved across Bermuda Hundred. Literally by the thousands, men fell from the ranks." John M. Christy of Company H, 45th USCT, remembered that "we marched all night till some of the boys gave out and lay down along the road and some throde their things away." Edward King Wightman, in a letter to his brother, described the ordeal of the 3rd New York:

> We…made an exhausting march…Late in the afternoon of the 28th of Sept. the 10th Corps left the Petersburg front and during the night crossed the Appomatox [sic] and James Rivers on pontoon bridges, to Deep Bottom. The distance was about twenty miles, and the march with knapsacks was so severe that hundreds of men halted and straggled on the way.[59]

A general in the 1st Division learned from his regimental surgeons that "they never saw so many men break down from sheer exhaustion as that night." Another officer observed, "Many who never fell out before dropped exhausted by the wayside." Colonel Galusha Pennypacker of the 97th Pennsylvania was not so kind in his assessment and complained of "unnecessary and disgraceful straggling during the first day's march." Brigadier General Terry and the vanguard of his 1st Division would not reach Deep Bottom until after midnight on the morning of the twenty-ninth. General Foster reported that he reached Deep Bottom at 1:30 a.m. The last units of the 2nd Division did not make their way across the pontoon bridge until thirty minutes later. Chaplain Hyde recalled, "It was half past two on the morning of the 29th when the commands reached their halting place, just beyond the redoubt." The regimental historian of the 24th Massachusetts reminisced that "after a long and tedious tramp we reached our old station at Deep Bottom at 2 o'clock in the morning of the 29th." A bedraggled Wightman stated that "[w]hen we stopped on the East [north] side of the James, early in the morning of the 29th, only forty men and two commissioned officers of the 3rd Regiment were present…Heartily tired, we threw ourselves upon the muddy ground and were allowed one hour, by the watch, for sleep."[60]

Edward Cook of Company H, 100th New York, wrote to his sister after this grueling ordeal and told her about "a very fatiguing march last night through woods and over bad roads, crossing the Appomattox & then the James river on pontoons we found ourselves at 2½ oclock this A.M. halted at Deep Bottom." He then sarcastically noted, "This does not look much like going to North Carolina." Still, if the weary and exhausted troops who had actually made it to Deep Bottom without breaking down thought that they were going to be afforded a chance to rest and refit before they were to be used in combat, they quickly learned that they were sadly mistaken. "We were allowed to sleep till half-past three," said one of Birney's worn-out men, "when we started for the front."[61]

Early on the morning of September 29, Captain McMurray recalled, "[W]e were astir, and before sunrise were on the march." Christian Fleetwood went about his morning routine: "Stirred up Regt. and, Knap[s]acks…Coffe [sic] boiled and line formed. Moved out & on."[62]

For many of these soldiers, this brief respite would provide their last sip of coffee.

Chapter 4

"UNFLINCHING HEROISM"

DUNCAN'S ASSAULT

As soon as Birney's lead units crossed the James, an ominous and morbid sight greeted them: "the Embalmer-General to the army, whose suggestive notices had greeted the eyes of each soldier as he marched to the front." A member of Butler's staff pointed out the obvious—that this could have a deleterious effect on the morale of the men—and the embalmer was finally told to find somewhere else to ply his trade.[63]

At first light, Terry's 1st Division of the 10th Corps, along with Paine, led the Union advance on the roads leading north from the Federal bridgehead at Deep Bottom. Skirmishers encountered and chased Confederate outposts across the Kingsland Road all the way to their main picket line north of Four Mile Creek. Lieutenant Nathan Edgerton of the 6th USCT recalled:

> We went forward about a mile without encountering the enemy; then our skirmishers came upon their pickets and lively firing began. The enemy, however, gave way almost immediately, falling back upon their reserves, and again on to their main line. Our skirmishers pursued so rapidly that we had to go at a double-quick to keep at proper supporting distance, and we were close upon their heels.

Colonel Clinton M. Winkler of the 4th Texas had been enjoying a brief respite with his wife when firing on the picket line was heard. Mrs. Winkler recalled her husband "hastily bidding me good-bye [with] sharp-shooting beginning to be heard." Confederate Edward Crockett of Company F, 4th

Texas Infantry, wrote in his diary, "The 29th, Thursday, all up and under arms at 4 o'clock, at early dawn. The rifles began to crack on the picket line…All is excitement now."[64]

Terry's Division moved out on the right, deploying in line of battle along the Kingsland Road. His men held the line east of Paine's Division with three brigades. Terry remembered this ground from the Second Battle of Deep Bottom, and accordingly, he deployed his men the same way they had been deployed on August 14, 1864—from right to left were Foster, Pond, Hawley and Osborn, followed up by William Birney's Brigade of United States Colored Troops. Plaisted's Brigade was posted on Terry's far right, with the right flank resting on a stream known as Four Mile Creek. Pond's Brigade deployed to the left of Plaisted's. Abbot's Brigade was next in line, to the left of Pond and Plaisted and to the right of Paine's Division.[65]

As the Rebel pickets continued to fall back, it became increasingly clear to the men of Paine's Division that their task would not be an easy one. The ground over which they would have to advance was strewn with obstacles, both natural and man-made. The chief natural obstacle was Four Mile Creek, which flowed on a roughly north–south axis past the New Market Road and through the trenches of the Texas Brigade. From there it flowed southward until it reached a wooded ravine just north of the Kingsland Road, where it branched out and ran east–west, roughly parallel to the New Market Road. Once they negotiated the ravine of Four Mile Creek, the ground in their front began to slope northward to the New Market Road and New Market Heights beyond. The heights ran for one mile from Signal Hill—just north of the New Market Road and directly in the path of Paine's oncoming men—east to Camp Holly and the redoubt of the 1st Rockbridge Artillery.

At this point, the relatively inexperienced Paine made a blunder that would lead to exceedingly high casualties for the lead units of his assault. If his division had kept pushing west once it had crossed the Kingsland Road, it would have encountered fewer obstacles and could have isolated the Confederates manning the New Market Line east of Four Mile Creek. Instead, Paine ordered Duncan's Brigade to halt and deploy his men in a double line of battle north of and parallel to the Kingsland Road. The 4th USCT would be in advance, with the 6th in support. Duncan's men then shifted to their right in order to close up any gaps between them and Terry's 10th Corps divisions. This placed Paine's Division directly in front of the portion of Four Mile Creek that ran from east to west, which added yet another obstacle that his men would have to overcome.[66]

With skirmishers remaining north of Grover Road, Colonel Draper had his men lie down in the woods near the Buffin House, since they had received no further orders. Paine's rear brigade—that of Holman—marched up, and Holman massed his men well behind the center of Duncan's thin line. It is unknown whether or not Paine had intended to use Holman's columns as a reserve in case Duncan encountered any trouble, since they were never committed once the fighting had begun. The only support Duncan's beleaguered troops would receive came from the men of the 2nd United States Colored Cavalry, who were unbrigaded and serving as dismounted skirmishers on Duncan's right.[67]

Paine's Division was on the left flank of the Union line of battle, north of the Kingsland Road close to the Buffin House. This line initially extended east and west along the Kingsland Road on a five-brigade front of about 2,350 yards. Duncan's Brigade of Paine's Division deployed to the left of Terry's Division near the Buffin House, supported by the brigades of Draper and Holman. The 22nd USCT deployed to cover the left flank of the battle line. The remainder of the 10th Corps was held in reserve in front of Deep Bottom, with some units in the vicinity of the Grover and Buffin Houses.

Brigadier General Robert S. Foster's 10th Corps Division was also held in reserve near Butler's headquarters at the Grover House. The overall situation, then, was that six of Paine's nine regiments and all thirteen of Foster's were held in reserve, waiting for things to play out. Paine's blunder led to a situation in which only one small brigade—1,100 officers and men, nearly half of whom were away serving as skirmishers—had the daunting task of taking a position that had defied two previous attempts to take it.[68]

With roughly 1,100 troops at his disposal to take care of the Rebels holding on to the New Market Line, Paine made yet another blunder: he selected only one brigade to storm the works. It seems as though Paine and Terry were not well aware as to what the other was doing, as Paine wrote shortly after the battle that "I waited a good while to hear Terry begin because I wanted him to draw some of the enemy away from me if he c[oul]d, but after waiting a good while and not hearing from Terry, I started my column." The orders came down, and the 3rd Brigade was ordered forward. Colonel Samuel A. Duncan's 3rd Brigade consisted of the 4th, 6th and 10th USCT—on paper, at least. In reality, all that Duncan had with him that day were two regiments numbering about 750 men. The 4th and 6th USCT had seen combat before, but the 10th was inexperienced and had been left behind at City Point.[69] They would form the tip of the spear in the push against the New Market Line.

In addition to the natural barrier formed by Four Mile Creek, the Confederates had created an even more lethal killing ground by building a series of obstacles known as slashing and chevaux-de-frise. In the days before barbed wire, wooden obstructions were used by both armies to accomplish the same goal—slow down the advance of the enemy long enough for them to be decimated by the small arms and artillery fire of the men behind the trenches. In front of the New Market Line, the first line of obstructions erected by the Rebels was referred to as "slashing," sometimes referred to as "an abatis of slashing." One war correspondent who found himself with the Army of the James during the fall of 1864 described the slashing in front of New Market Heights as follows:

> By this process called "slashing," the trees are felled outwards, at right angles to the work, narrow belts only being left in the hollows of a stream to cover the retreat of pickets or skirmishers. The enemy, therefore, is obliged to clamber through a tangled jungle of boughs which face him, without being at all sheltered from the withering fire of the defenders of the work.[70]

An officer in the 6th USCT described the slashing, stating that the Rebels were "posted behind a line of earthworks, protected in front by a dense growth of light brushwood, lopped down so that the stumps and trees yet cling together, forming a tangled network of limbs and trunks difficult to penetrate."[71]

If Duncan's men could negotiate their way through this tangled mess, the next line of wooden impediments was called chevaux-de-frise. These structures were made by sharpening the ends of trees and connecting them together through large logs to form a portable defense system. Lieutenant Nathan Edgerton, the adjutant of the 6th USCT, recalled that "the earthwork immediately in front of us was strengthened by an abatis extending along its entire face. This had in front of it a sluggish stream with slimy banks and mossy bottom, about four yards wide."[72] Another member of the 6th, Captain John McMurray, remembered:

> The field across which we were marching was possibly twenty rods [one rod equals five and a half feet] in width...From the edge of the wood the ground descended slightly towards the enemy's line of works. Between the far edge of the field and the line of rifle pits had been a strip of woods eight or ten yards wide, through which ran a small stream, parallel with the line of works.

Captain John McMurray of the 6th USCT was still haunted by what he saw on the morning of September 29, 1864, when he began publishing his reminiscences in his hometown newspaper fifty-two years after the battle. *From* Recollections of a Colored Troop.

Men of the 4th and 6th USCT encountered more Confederate pickets at the edge of the heavily wooded ravine through which Four Mile Creek meandered. Duncan's two forlorn regiments crossed the fields and, reaching the edge of the abatis, paused to dress their lines, "with as much care and accuracy as though we had been on parade." Not a shot came from the foe crouching behind the earthworks, which caused Captain McMurray to imagine that the Confederates probably "looked on with great interest thinking no doubt what a lot of fools we were." Looking back on the experience, McMurray mused, "In contemplating since the results of that day, I have been led to see the wisdom of God in concealing from man what is before him." If he had any inkling of the maelstrom he was about to march into, "I would have been entirely unfitted for the duties of the day."[73]

About this time, Ben Butler himself rode up to the troops to exhort them. The general recalled that he found them "with guns at 'right shoulder shift,'" which signaled that they were ready to step off. Pointing at the New Market Line, Butler cried out, "That work must be taken by the weight of your column; no shot must be fired." To prevent Duncan's foot soldiers from stopping to fire, which would stall out the attack, Butler ordered his men to remove the percussion caps from their rifles. Without these caps, the muskets that the soldiers carried could not fire. They would have to rush across the open ground and carry the works at the point of the bayonet, after which they would be permitted to cap their rifles and open fire. Summoning his powers of oration that had developed over decades

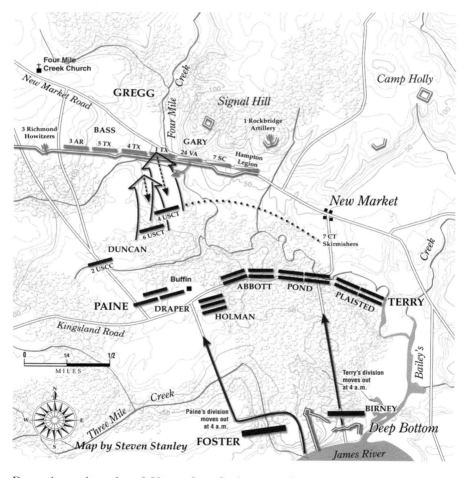

Duncan's assault, at about 5:30 a.m. *Steven Stanley, cartographer.*

as a lawyer and politician, Butler then exhorted his men: "Your cry, when you charge, will be, 'Remember Fort Pillow!'" Finally, Duncan bellowed, "'Forward!' and as one man we plunged into the slashing."[74] It was roughly 5:30 a.m.

Duncan's two regiments deployed in a skirmish line about two hundred yards long, the 4th USCT leading and the 6th USCT echeloned to the left rear. Even more incredibly, Duncan and the other line officers followed close behind, mounted on their horses. Major Augustus Boernstein of the 4th wrote shortly after the battle, "We did not dismount during the whole fight until our horses were shot. If we had succeeded in taking the Rebel line we would have been captured, every one of us."[75]

Surging across the hollow, the black troops drove in the pickets and charged the rifle pits south of and parallel to the New Market Road. One Texan later recalled that "hostilities had begun on the picket line at three o'clock, and at daylight the Texas Brigade…was busily engaged in slaughtering negroes for breakfast." William G. Hinson of the 7th South Carolina Cavalry recorded in his diary for the twenty-ninth that he and his fellow horse soldiers had "rushed in [to the] breastworks to find our skirmish line falling in hard pressed by Negro troops." Another Rebel reminisced that "in a few moments we were all heavily engaged, the negroes crossed the second line of abates [sic], & in to the first, when the fight raged for a few minutes, men firing on them at about 25 steps."[76]

Joseph Polley of the 4th Texas recalled that "the fog was so thick as to render large objects, a hundred feet distant, indistinguishable. All that could be seen through the dense fog enveloping us was what appeared to be a moving black wall a hundred feet away." Colonel Duncan remembered the fog that morning as well, relating how he saw his men "disappear, as they entered the fog that enwrapped them like a mantle of death." As the pickets of the Texas Brigade begin to pour back into their main line, they shouted out in warning, "Niggers boys, niggers!" to let their compatriots know that what they derisively termed a "coon fight" was about to begin.[77]

Orlando T. Hanks of the 1st Texas relayed a story about a loss that would make any soldier cringe—the loss of his breakfast:

> *One beautiful still morning about sunrise we heard cheering away in the distance on the James. It was so faint it sounded like little school boys at play. We were preparing our breakfast and did not pay much attention to it. I was boiling for myself and mess, a pot of sweet potatoes. Just then the hieing was nearer. Some of the boys remarked that those wretches were coming one and all on us. Twas but a little while our pickets began to pup away and*

gave them a pretty stiff fight. But it was of no use. They were being driven by a strong line of battle of the enemy. By this time our officers began to give orders to fall in line and get into the breastworks. Into them we went. I carried my pot of potatoes. I had not time to eat them and less appetite. Likewise I left them sitting there and they are there now as far as I know.[78]

While the Confederates could only draw on about 2,900 men to defend the New Market Line, Duncan's 750 men were outnumbered at the point of attack. It seems that many of the Rebel troops were incensed once they found out that black soldiers were attacking them. A Texan by the name of D.H. Hamilton recalled, "Whatever [Grant's] purpose [for using black troops] it was like flaunting a red flag before a mad bull. No man in our old Brigade would have retreated from, or surrendered to Niggers. When they charged…the fun began." Another member of the Lone Star State recalled that "the word was passed along the line that they were negroes and to give them lead. Every fellow shot with as much precision as if they were at a shooting match." Writing on October 3, Paine marveled in a letter home that "there were not many men in the reb line…but where I assaulted there were as many as the works w[oul]d hold. They had a signal tower which overlooked everything and [which] enabled them to concentrate to meet me." Historian Richard J. Sommers estimated that there were 1,800 Confederate soldiers in the works directly in front of Duncan's Brigade.[79]

As the 6th USCT struggled toward the Confederate line, the unit's adjutant, Lieutenant Nathan Edgerton, was finding it difficult to maneuver through the swampy terrain on horseback. When he came up the streambed of Four

Lieutenant John B. Johnson was "shot through the right arm near the wrist" during Duncan's assault—one of many young officers to fall dead or wounded at New Market Heights. *Author's collection.*

Mile Creek, he "jumped from my horse and threw the reins to the orderly, for I was sure the horse would be unable to get across owing to the marshy nature of the ground. The reins had hardly left my hand when the horse went down, shot dead from the opposite bank." Continuing on foot, Edgerton "got over the stream," and climbing up to the other side, he "found a level space of ground thickly covered with our dead and wounded." Among this bloody heap, he found the body of Lieutenant Frank Meyers, with the regiment's flag gripped in his lifeless fingers. Edgerton grabbed the flag and tried to advance the colors up to the forward-most point of advance. He stumbled forward, tripping over vines that clogged the ground, and "looked down…to see why I could not lift" the flag. To his horror, he discovered that his hand was "covered in blood, and perfectly powerless, and the flag staff lying in two pieces." Summoning all the strength he could muster, Edgerton sheathed his sword and "took the flag with its broken staff and reached the abatis." For his actions that day, Edgerton would be awarded the Medal of Honor.[80]

Working one's way through the abatis was a dangerous business—the Confederates now leaped on top of their earthworks and blazed away. The Colored Troops had little chance to retaliate, and men fell with every forward step. Captain McMurray passed his first sergeant, who had taken a Minié ball in the leg, and then he ran into another of his soldiers named Emanuel Patterson. Captain McMurray had seen Patterson on the twenty-eighth when the young private had complained that he was too sick to go on the march. After being sent to the surgeon, Patterson was ordered back to the front. Again, on the morning of the twenty-ninth, Patterson complained that he was too sick to go into battle, and Captain McMurray accompanied him to the surgeon personally to see if the soldier could be excused for the day. The doctor once again said that he could not. Young Emanuel was forced into the fight, and the next time McMurray saw him, Patterson "was shot in the abdomen, so that his bowels all gushed out, forming a mass larger than my hat, seemingly, which he was holding up with his clasped hands, to keep them from falling at his feet." Sitting down to write his memoir in 1916, that sight still haunted McMurray, and even as an old man, he lamented, "I wish I had taken the responsibility of saying to him that he could remain in the rear."[81]

Led on by the officers and NCOs who were still standing, a number of the USCTs picked their way through the felled timber, struggled through the chevaux-de-frise and gained the trenches held by the 1st Texas. As the men moved closer to the works, the cannons of the 1st Rockbridge Artillery opened a lethal fire that tore gaping holes in the ranks of Duncan's oncoming soldiers. Remembered J.H. Goulding:

The 4th and 6th regiments lead and as they rush down the incline, receive the concentrated fire of the whole rebel division. The crash of small arms is terrific, a constant roll with the heavier discharges of artillery breaking in like the bass notes of some mighty organ. The air seems full of missiles, hissing above, around and with deadly intent at each one of us. Man after man with the colors goes down, and officer after officer as they snatch the falling staff from stricken falling arms. With shouts and cries, with deep drawn breath and gasps and choking heart-throbs we plunge on and on, men dropping suddenly or thrown whirling or doubled up as they were struck. Now we reach the brook and are tearing our way through the brush. What wild music the bullets sing as we force our way along! "Keep on boys." My God, see them reel and stagger, and yet still keep coming on. The dense masses of the rebels, their yellow works, are in plain sight; we hear their shouts and cheers, their pitiless, incessant, withering volleys. Surging up to the parapet, our men leap the low, newly made lines and black and white meet, hand to hand, no longer as master and slave.[82]

Sergeant Major Christian Fleetwood and the members of his twelve-man color guard in the 4th USCT were having a rough time of it as well, since Rebel soldiers loved to pick off any soldier carrying the regimental colors.

Col. Joseph Hiram Goulding.

Shown later in life, Joseph Goulding had only completed two years as a cadet at Norwich University when he was commissioned a first lieutenant in the 6th USCT. He would leave behind one of the most vivid accounts of the Battle of New Market Heights. *From* Norwich University, 1819–1911.

Fleetwood later recalled, "It was a deadly hailstorm of bullets, sweeping men down as hailstones sweep the leaves from the trees." Fleetwood noticed that Sergeant Alfred B. Hilton, who carried the regimental colors of the 4th USCT, went down screaming, "Boys, save the colors!" as he fell. Fleetwood watched as his friend, Corporal Charles Veal, unhesitatingly picked up the flag. In a matter of seconds, another member of the color guard was hit, and Fleetwood stepped forward to rescue the national colors of the 4th. As he continued to advance, Fleetwood observed:

> [I]t was very evident that there was too much work cut out for our regiments…We struggled through the two lines of abatis, a few getting through the palisades, but it was sheer madness, and those of us who were able I had to get out as best we could. Reaching the line of our reserves and no commissioned officer being in sight, I rallied the survivors around the flag, rounding up at first eighty-five men and three commissioned officers.

The flag that Fleetwood rescued had more than twenty-two bullet holes in it, and the staff had been sliced in half from the sheer volume of the Confederate rifle and artillery fire. For their actions that day, Sergeant Hilton (who survived his wound), Corporal Veal and Sergeant Major Fleetwood were all awarded Medals of Honor.[83]

Sergeant Major Thomas C. Hawkins of the 6th USCT was credited with rescuing the regimental colors during Duncan's assault even though he had received three wounds. For his actions that day, Hawkins received the Medal of Honor. *Library of Congress.*

Meanwhile, the color guard of the 6th USCT was having problems of a similar kind. As the 6th was subjected to severe musket and artillery fire, the color guard was shot to pieces, and Sergeant Major Thomas C. Hawkins was credited with rescuing the regimental colors before withdrawing with the rest of Duncan's Brigade. Hawkins did not survive unscathed, however—he was wounded in the arm, hip and foot. Hawkins's friend, Christian Fleetwood, later wrote that "his recovery from these fearful wounds was deemed hopeless." Alexander Kelly faced a similar ordeal when he rescued the national colors of the 6th. He later recalled:

> *After the color guard was all either killed or wounded and our colors falling inside the second line of abities [sic] we got orders to retire seeing the flag was being left I seized them and carried them to rear where I rallied the few remaining men…I advanced in the atack with 35 men out of which only 10 was left for duty.*[84]

Solomon T. Blessing of the Texas Brigade recalled that the Federals "were delayed somewhat by the abatis, but some, however, came through the gap left for the creek and got into our works." The ranks of Duncan's two regiments continued to melt away as the Rebels blazed away. Lieutenant James H. Wilkes of the 4th USCT would never forget how "the whole line seemed to wilt down under the fearful fire which was then poured into us. The line was growing too weak and too thin to make an assault. It began to waiver." Yet on they came. Colonel Duncan went down with four wounds. Colonel John Ames of the 6th USCT took overall command on the field once Duncan was wounded. Inheriting an impossible task, Ames, "his long mustache dripping with blood from a cut across the forehead," took account of the situation and turned to a nearby officer. "Captain," he asked, "don't you think we had better fall back? We haven't enough force to take this line, and if we remain here we will probably all be killed." He then turned to his soldiers and shouted, "We must have more help, boys, before we try that. Fall back."[85]

Goulding described the flight back:

> *Desperately turning, back the survivors go; the enemy's fire rekindling and adding many to the fallen as we seek for safety the shelter of the crest so far, far away. We gain it at last, breathless, and yet, reforming, the men beg to be led in again, declaring they can and will effect a lodgment in the works.*

In less than an hour, Duncan's two regiments had been repulsed with terrible losses. The woes of Duncan's Brigade had been compounded by

The remnants of the flag that Christian Fleetwood rescued at New Market Heights. This flag was presented to the 4th USCT by the African American ladies of Baltimore, Maryland, in 1863. After the morning assault, Major Augustus S. Boernstein recalled that the flag's staff was cut in half, and he counted more than twenty-two bullet holes in the flag itself. *Maryland Historical Society.*

Paine's errors. Holman's Brigade, posted in support of Duncan, held its ground south of Four Mile Creek, anxiously awaiting orders from Paine to advance. Captain Albert Janes of the 22nd USCT stated that while Duncan's men were attacking, Holman's men had "conformed to the movements of the line"—and that is all.[86] While the forlorn hope of Duncan's assault was taking place, the 2nd Brigade under Colonel Draper had pressed cautiously ahead toward a small stream floating into Four Mile Creek but could gain no advantage before they were called east to help shield Ames's retreat, with the 22nd USCT taking their place.

Terry's Division was also of no help to Duncan's troops. Colonel Joseph Abbott's Brigade formed a battle line along the Kingsland Road and threw forward the 7th Connecticut as skirmishers. These videttes crossed Four Mile Creek and engaged General Gary's pickets. Terry's limited mission and failure to support Paine is underscored by Colonel Abbot's concern about the security of his left wing, where enraged Confederates had followed Duncan's retreating men to gather up firearms, plunder the dead and, in some cases, kill the wounded.[87] A Union officer later recalled that "many of our wounded and all of our dead…were left in the hands of the

Brigadier General Alfred C. Terry's failure to come to the support of Paine's men during the initial minutes of the attack on New Market Heights ensured that Duncan's Brigade would receive no support in its forlorn charge against the enemy's entrenchments. *Library of Congress.*

rebels," and another officer stated that he had witnessed some of Gregg's men killing the wounded.[88]

When Colonel Duncan was convalescing from the four wounds he had received that morning, he had time to proudly reflect on the performance of his brigade that morning. Writing to his wife, he exclaimed, "Ah! give me the Thunder-heads & Black hearts after all. They fought splendidly that morning, facing the red tempest of death with unflinching heroism."[89]

Duncan's Brigade carried roughly 750 men into that fight that cool September morning. By the time the charge was complete, 387 of those men had been killed, wounded or captured. The 6th USCT lost 57 percent of its total strength, and Company D of that regiment lost 87 percent of its men. In the 4th USCT, Lieutenant William A. Appleton, Sergeant Major Christian A. Fleetwood and Sergeants Charles Veal and Alfred Hilton would be awarded Medals of Honor. In the 6th, Lieutenant Nathan Edgerton, Sergeant Major Thomas C. Hawkins and First Sergeant Alexander Kelly would receive the same honor.[90]

Mercifully, Duncan's men had done their bit and would not be called on to fight again on this day. Many of their black compatriots would not be so fortunate.

Chapter 5

"THIRTY MINUTES OF TERRIBLE SUSPENSE"

DRAPER'S ASSAULT

While Duncan's Brigade was being shattered against the fortifications in front of Bass's Texans, the men of William Birney's Brigade had been held back. From their vantage point, they could see their comrades mown down by the torrent of lead that the Rebels were able to bring to bear against them. Soldiers in the 29th Connecticut (Colored) had a front-row seat to watch their fellow blacks fall under the immensity of the Rebel fire. "[W]ee Could look ahead & see the men fall one after another," remembered Corporal Joseph O. Cross. One of Cross's compatriots left a vivid account of what he saw that day:

> *These scenes would have made your heart sore. Dear reader, the wounded and dying scattered over the battlefield thick, the hurrying to and fro of the physicians and the nurses; the prayers and groans and cries of the wounded, the explosion of bombs, the whizzing of bullets, the cracking of rifles; you would have thought that the very forces of hell had been let loose. And, indeed, it was a hell, the horrors of which no one could ever forget.*

In the end, the men of the 29th Connecticut counted themselves fortunate to be spared the same fate as Duncan's Brigade.[91]

Meanwhile, Butler conferred with Birney and Kautz at a nearby house to see what progress was being made. As he rode to this impromptu council of war, he came across some of Duncan's wounded soldiers who were on their way to seek treatment and "inquired kindly whether they were much

The 29th Regiment Connecticut Infantry (Colored) on parade. Although the 29th was held in reserve, it saw its fellow black soldiers take dreadful casualties at New Market Heights. *Library of Congress.*

hurt, praising those who had carried their rifles with them off the field." The wounded soldiers smiled when they recognized their general and saluted smartly, informing him that they were going to be fine. Butler then proceeded to his rendezvous with Birney and Kautz. An observer noted that Butler sat in the center of the group, "wearing a small French cap… known as his 'fighting cap,'" and that Kautz sat on his right, with Birney at his left. They could hear the intense battle raging nearby, and when a courier rode up to inform them that Fort Harrison had fallen, the meeting quickly broke up.[92]

During the lull in fighting, Gregg had seen that the threat to Fort Harrison was much greater, since that bastion was closer to Richmond than the New Market Line. He sent a courier to the 17th Georgia, under DuBose, which was close to where the fight was raging. Captain Judge Martin of Company

Butler's headquarters at Chaffin's Farm. *Library of Congress*.

G stated that "a courier dashed up and said that the enemy were attacking the Texas Brigade, and I was ordered to go back and assist them." A.C. Jones of the Texas Brigade remembered that "a swift messenger informed us that Fort Harrison, one mile away, was in danger." While one Confederate stated that the courier arrived "just after sunrise," which was at 6:08 a.m., a soldier in the 1st Texas wrote in his diary that the orders to move in that direction did not come until 8:00 a.m. To further confuse the matter, Captain Martin of the 17th Georgia recalled that "just as this attack [Duncan's assault] had been repulsed a courier came down and told us to reinforce Battery Harrison." While some historians maintain that Bass and Gary "obviously discussed the order and route of withdrawal of the regiments...in the event the line had to be evacuated," such an assertion is purely speculative, and there is no evidence to suggest that the two commanders met. In any event, the

Confederates in the New Market Line could not have gotten very far in their preparations to evacuate the line when they were suddenly hit with another Federal assault.[93]

As the wreckage of Duncan's shattered units trickled back, it was clear that the Confederates still clung to their bastion and could fend off similar attacks all day long with little or no damage to themselves at all. Nonetheless, within minutes the orders from Birney came down—Paine's Division would once again assail the New Market Line. This time, Paine's 2nd Brigade under Draper would carry the load while Terry's Division was to advance against the rifle pits defended by Gary's dismounted troopers on the Confederate left. This particular brigade had been ready to attack along with Duncan's men, but according to Draper, "[W]e were directed to lie down and wait for further orders." The brigade then "advanced immediately across the open field, leaving Ruffin's house on our left. On this field we received a skirmish fire from the woods." While this inconsequential skirmishing was taking place, Colonel Draper "received an order from Brigadier-General Paine to move my brigade to the right, as 'we were getting the worst of it there.' We immediately moved by the right flank and again by the left (by the proper evolutions), and formed at the ravine, where the troops lay down in line." With the men formed up and ready to go, an onlooking reporter noticed that "every man looked like a soldier while inflexible determination was depicted upon every countenance."[94]

Finally, the order to advance came down. At least three regiments, totaling about 1,300 men, would be going in this time—the 5th, 36th and 38th USCT, in that order—and Draper's left flank was to be protected by skirmishers from the 22nd USCT. Before the men of the 5th USCT got underway, Lieutenant Colonel Giles Shurtleff addressed them, stating, "If you are brave soldiers, the stigma…denying you full and equal rights of citizenship shall…be swept away and your race forever rescued from the cruel prejudice and oppression which have been upon you from the foundation of the government." Draper had the sense to mass his men for this assault, instead of spreading them out in a long, thin line like Duncan had. He ordered the brigade to attack in line of regimental columns by divisions, which meant that they would hit the Southerners with a column six companies wide and ten ranks deep. This compact formation allowed for a much stronger punch, and the depth of the column ensured that if the men in front encountered any trouble, there would be sufficient force behind them to continue the momentum of the attack. But would it be enough?[95]

As the brigade stepped off, the men first had to negotiate a belt of young pine trees before wheeling into an open plain fronting the Confederate works. It was now roughly 7:30 a.m., and the sun had risen. As the morning fog that had enshrouded Duncan's men was burned away, the attacking USCTs could see their dead and wounded comrades littering the ground in front of them—an ominous portent of what lay ahead. Not only did they come upon the casualties of the 4th and 6th USCT, they also encountered the very same obstacle that had impeded their progress: the deadly

Major General David Bell Birney was one of the best fighting generals that the Union war effort produced. He pulled himself out of his sickbed to command the 10th Corps on September 29, 1864, but the strain of the next few weeks resulted in his leaving for home. He died three weeks after the battle. *Library of Congress*.

accurate artillery fire of the Rockbridge Artillery. The black troops surged too far to the west, and the units farthest on the left were crowded into the swampy ground near Four Mile Creek. When they were forced to cross the east–west portion of the creek, this "broke the charge, as the men had to wade the run or stream and reform on the bank." A sense of confusion pervaded the attackers, and as they drew closer to the slashing, they took what cover could be found behind the fallen tree trunks.[96]

While confusion reigned and the black troops under Draper's command pushed forward, it seems that some of the men remembered the battle cry that Butler had told them to raise when they attacked. One offended Confederate wrote in his diary entry for September 29, "[A]s they came up they shouted remember 'Fort Pillow' & give the Rebels no quarter. This stirred up our men and everybody seemed mad for the first time, & some of the boys on the left jumped over the works, and formed across their flanks line and enfiladed them." Another soldier in Bass's command remembered that "our trusty rifles prevailed by willing hands & brave hearts, pour[ing]

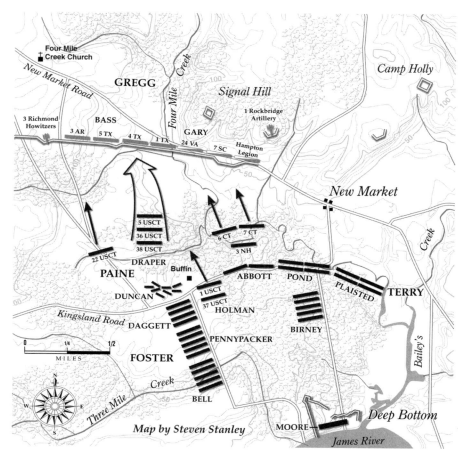

Draper's assault, 7:30 a.m. *Steven Stanley, cartographer.*

swift destruction into their ranks." Supporting these accounts, an officer in the 17th Georgia wrote that "the Texans…killed niggers galore."[97]

When the men of the 5th USCT had emerged from Four Mile Creek, Lieutenant Joseph Scroggs stated that "we finally struggled through the last swamp and up the last bank, to find ourselves alone and unsupported, exposed to an enfilading fire of artillery and musketry in front which now for the first began to tell upon our ranks with murderous effect." With Draper's men gone to ground, they did precisely what they had been told not to do: they capped their muskets and opened fire on the enemy. Colonel Draper knew that it was suicidal madness to engage an entrenched foe in firefight, and he began running to every junior officer he could find, screaming at them to rally their men and get them moving forward again. William Hart of the 36th USCT (Draper's old regiment) recalled seeing him during this crisis:

> *I will remember seeing…Draper in that critical moment, when our line waivered and seemed about to fall back and abandon the attempt to carry the rebel works at the point of the bayonet, he was standing upon a slight eminence, sword in hand, every vestige of color had left his face, but he was cognizant of everything going on about him, and fully realized the gravity of the situation.*

As more and more soldiers were picked off or ravaged by the shower of shrapnel raining down on them, the instinct for self-preservation kicked in, and many men ignored the pleas of their officers, thinking that it was safer to stay behind cover and fire at the Rebel works.[98]

Once again it looked as if Butler's sable warriors were doomed to be sacrificed by his subordinates' inflexibility. To Draper's right, Abbott's Brigade moved forward in the vanguard of Terry's Division. When they encountered Four Mile Creek, they were enfiladed by cannons of the Rockbridge Artillery to their front right. Colonel Alfred Rockwell of the 6th Connecticut wrote that "when the order to advance was received I moved across the open field, through a deep ravine, and halted upon the edge of the open field in front of the enemy's works. During this time we were subjected to an enfilading artillery fire, which, however, occasioned me no loss." Another member of the 6th recalled that "musketry fire was very rapid and the shells exploded with terrible force over the heads of the gallant soldiers." Captain S.S. Atwell of the 7th Connecticut reported that the enemy works in his front were well manned. Abbott pushed the 3rd New Hampshire forward to bolster his line, but this did nothing more than to make Gary's troopers hunker down in their rifle pits. Major James F. Randlett of the 3rd reported what happened next:

> *Colonel Abbott instructed me to advance my line as rapidly as possible, reporting success to him, exercising my own discretion. When in full view of enemy and his works, 500 yards across the opening, I advanced a light line and drew from the enemy the disposition of his forces. Finding my line flanked on the left by works similar to those in my front, and discovering that he was reenforcing the flank, I ordered my men to lie down, the advantage of the rolling ground being such as to entirely protect them from his infantry while his artillery played over us into the ravine.*[99]

Meanwhile, the men of the 22nd USCT over on the left were getting shelled as they made their way through a "dense tangle of underbrush and felled trees into an open plain." As they crossed the plain, a few were picked off by Confederate sharpshooters. Beyond the woods, they encountered the portion of the line manned by the 3rd Arkansas. The skirmishers halted in front of the abatis, while Holman brought up the 1st and 37th USCT. Draper was none too pleased at this lack of support, writing in his report that "the Twenty-second U.S. Colored Troops were to skirmish on our left. This they did for awhile, but did not continue to the works."[100]

While Draper's men were pinned down in the slashing, casualties piled up at an alarming rate. Lieutenant Scroggs left a vivid account of what happened to his men in his diary:

I had given up the hope of returning alive from this "very jaws of death," and thought that it was only left for me to die facing the enemy...The utter hopelessness of succeeding pervaded the mind of every one when they had time to think. I did not lie down as that position offered no security, and I seen the companies one by one commencing on the left to rise to their feet run a few yards and then as if recollecting themselves, walk deliberately from the field. I seen a man of my own Co....get up, step out a dozen yards in front of the line and cooly fire his piece at the enemy, then slowly follow the Co. from the ground. I seen a Sergeant who had received three different wounds crying because the battalion would not go farther. I seen men tenderly and slowly carrying their wounded captain...off that field of death, and also their wounded comrades, from where to delay was almost madness. I seen all this and more, and no man dare hereafter say

Lieutenant Joseph Scroggs was an Ohio farmer who had served as an enlisted man in the early days of the Civil War before applying to be an officer with the Bureau of Colored Troops. His diary provides intense descriptions of Draper's assault. *Rob Lyon.*

aught in my presence against the bravery and soldierly qualities of the colored soldiers.

Lieutenant Elliot Grabill, also of the 5th USCT, recalled in a letter written to his wife that "the shells were shrieking around so that I was afraid one should tear me to pieces…We pushed forward…right up against the rebel works, through abatis, through brush, through shell and shot." He concluded by observing that "the men suffered heavily. Poor fellows! They fought splendidly."[101]

Repeatedly wounded, Lieutenant Colonel Shurtleff refused to leave his men. In the 36th, two months' fever had left Draper's brother-in-law, Lieutenant Richard Andrews, "scarcely able to walk" and excused from duty, but he "rode to the thicket, dismounted, and charged to the swamp, where he was shot through the leg." Just beyond, a bullet struck the arm of Lieutenant Edwin C. Gaskill, who "rushed in front of his regiment, and, waving his sword, called on the men to follow" him from the marshes. Nearby fell Lieutenant James B. Backup, who had been excused from duty because of lameness and who "hobbled in as far as the swamp" and fell while leading his company forward. An orderly with blood flowing from a serious neck wound not only remained but, within minutes, charged the enemy lines as well. There, too, Lieutenant Samuel B. Bancroft of the 38th fell, shot in the hip, but he "crawled forward on his hands and knees, waving his sword and calling on the men to follow."

After what Draper called "thirty minutes of terrible suspense," the officers under his command were able to rally their men and get them moving again. With a shout that went up from one end of the line to the other, the black soldiers stopped firing and leapt to their feet. With their muskets in one hand, they began weaving their way through the slashing, high-stepping over the logs and avoiding the tree stumps if at all possible. After breaking through the fallen trunks, Draper's men swarmed through the chevaux-de-frise, and "with exultant cheers the column swept forward over the parapet, and occupied the coveted prize." As they did, a Confederate officer trying to inspire his men also leapt up onto the parapet and shouted out, "Hurrah, my brave men!" Rushing to meet him was Private James Gardiner of the 36th USCT. Seeing the Rebel officer, Gardiner ran ahead of the advancing column, shot the officer "and then ran the bayonet through his body to the muzzle."

One of Gardiner's comrades, Corporal Miles James, received a ghastly wound to his right arm shortly thereafter. The wound required "immediate

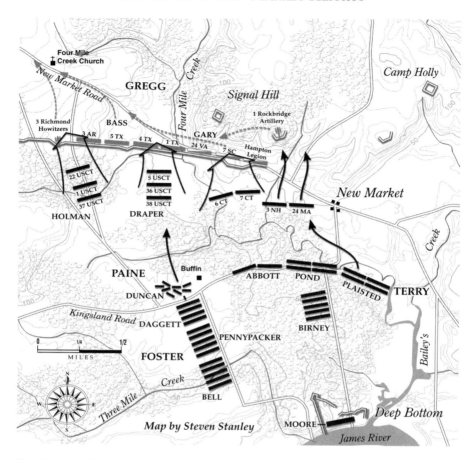

Breakthrough, 8:30 a.m. *Steven Stanley, cartographer.*

amputation," but even still, James "loaded and discharged his piece with one hand and urged his men forward." Cornelius Garner of Company B, 38th USCT, also received a slight wound during the charge but happily recalled years later: "I fit…wid de ole 38th regiment. We had colored sojers an' white officers. We licked de 'federate good an' made 'em [retreat] up to a place called Chaff's farm. Never will I fergit dat battle. It come on a Thursday, Sept. 29, 1864."

Draper would later complain that "in this assault we had no supports."[102]

Farther west, the 22nd USCT, noticing that the Rebels were pulling out, charged the works in its front, "driving the enemy in confusion from them." When the men pushed through the earthworks and emerged on the New Market Road, part of Holman's Brigade wheeled to the west and pushed along the works toward the McCoul House. As the Federals pushed farther in this direction, the 3rd Richmond Howitzers was forced to limber up and make a hasty retreat. One member of the Howitzers recorded in his diary that "when the enemy pierced our lines near the McCoul House our first section engaged them until it was compelled to retire for want of proper support—our infantry force being very weak. This section moved towards Richmond." After the cannoneers pulled out, Colonel Holman then called for a halt and ordered his men to regroup and await further instructions.[103]

The men of the 1st Rockbridge Artillery abandoned their cannon emplacement as Colonel Abbott's reinforced skirmish line saw that Draper's men had "commenced a rigorous attack" on its left and moved out into the open field that it had been so hesitant to venture into earlier. When the dismounted cavalry troopers under Gary saw this happening, they called for their horses to be brought up and joined the artillery in full retreat. Charles Crosland, who served as Gary's courier and clerk, remembered that trooper Will Simmons "jumped upon the works and swore he would have one good shot, when a rifle ball took him between the eyes and he fell backward dead. We lost a good many men here and were driven pell-mell back."

Contrary to other Confederate accounts of an orderly withdrawal toward Fort Harrison, Crosland bluntly stated that "[w]e ran in a panic for the line of works farther back commanded by Fort Harrison." Crosland was

Born a free man in Gloucester, Virginia, Private James Daniel Gardiner was a member of Company I, 36th USCT, when he stormed into the Confederate lines and bayoneted a Confederate officer who was trying to rally his men. Gardiner received the Medal of Honor for his heroism that day. *Library of Congress.*

not alone in his sentiment. William G. Hinson of the 7th South Carolina Cavalry described being "routed" in his diary and saw from his vantage point that the Yankees "broke through our right and left, which caused our hasty retreat under a heavy fire to the second line of breastworks." Edward Moore wryly quipped that "on the principle that the chased dog is generally the fleetest," the Rockbridge Artillery beat a hasty retreat. The harried artillerists and cavalrymen were the last Confederates to pull out of the New Market Line and join the rest of the column on its flight to safety.[104]

At roughly 8:30 p.m., General Foster's Division moved to the support of Draper, but by the time he reached the front, the fighting was over. He therefore moved to the vanguard of the 10th Corps as it prepared to push up the New Market Road toward Richmond. When news of the Federal success reached army headquarters at the Grover House, Butler dashed off a message to Grant stating that Birney's men had "taken the main line of works at the signal tower, New Market Heights, which commands the road and is advancing." Paine's Division had spearheaded the attack and stormed the New Market Line and had suffered "considerable loss" according to Butler's missive. At about the same time, "the signal flag of [Birney's] corps was seen ascending the knoll, and announced the capture of the Newmarket Heights."[105] The battle was finally over.

As was the case in Duncan's regiments, the casualties suffered by Draper's Brigade were horrific. Upon checking his rolls, he learned that of the 1,300 men he took into battle, he lost more than 400 men. The 5th USCT reported that total casualties from all of the fighting on the twenty-ninth totaled 28 killed, 8 officers and 177 men wounded and 23 missing. Joseph Scroggs recorded in his diary that "on getting my Co. [H] together I found I had lost 18 in killed and wounded, that cut [to] 50 the number I started with in the morning." The 36th USCT reported 22 men killed and 5 officers and 102 men wounded. The 38th USCT reported 1 officer and 16 men killed and 2 officers and 92 men wounded.

Reactions to the fight that had just taken place were mixed. A few Confederates could concede that the African American troops whom they had just fought did indeed behave like soldiers and, by implication, men. J.D. Pickens of the 1st Texas opined that "in my opinion, no troops to that time had fought us with more bravery than did those negroes." Pickens seemed to think that their valor was wasted, however—"I am sure there were several hundred dead negroes left on the field. The dead almost dammed up [Four Mile] Creek at one place. We certainly repulsed them with great slaughter."

Colonel Winkler of the 4th Texas wrote to his wife that "the sight I witnessed of dead negroes and white Federal officers was sickening in the extreme." Not every member of the Texas Brigade felt so kindly, however. Thomas C. McCarty bitterly recorded in his diary that "our men now have a perfect contempt for negro soldiers. It is almost a pity to put such things into battle," while another coldly calculated that "we killed in our front about a million dollars worth of niggers, at current prices."[106]

As the sound of the firing drifted farther west, the men of Duncan's Brigade came back to the front to see what had happened to their fellow comrades who had not returned earlier that morning. While looking for survivors, Lieutenant Joseph Goulding found one of the many members of the regiment's color guard who had been shot down during the assault. He sadly recalled:

> *Going over the field after the fight, we found the color sergeant of the 4th with both legs shattered by a round shot. He had crawled twenty yards to get out of the way of the rebs as they sprang over upon our wounded. His first question was, "Have we taken the works?" "Yes, sergeant, we have." He raised himself up to a sitting position while his mangled limbs hung by shreds of flesh, swung his hat over his head, gave a cheer for the colored brigade, and fell back gasping upon the turf. Tenderly laying him in the shade, we revived him with a little water, and after an inquiry as to whether he could live, which was answered doubtfully, he said faintly, "Well, I carried my colors up to the works, and I did my duty, didn't I?"[107]*

When the men of Daggett's Brigade came up, they were astounded at the number of casualties that littered the ground in front of the New Market Line. Edward King Wightman of the 3rd New York in Daggett's Brigade wrote in a letter home that "when we reached the turnpike…the works had been carried by colored troops, and the slaughtered negroes lay piled in heaps in front of them." Chaplain Hyde of the 112th New York stated that "the ground over which [the USCTs] passed in the charge was strewn with the slain, and the wounded soon filled a large plantation house in the rear, and the large enclosure surrounding it." George Stowits of the 100th New York later wrote that "we could have walked on their dead bodies from the outer to the inner side of the abatis without touching soil, so thick were they strewn in that deadly charge."[108]

Yet it was Benjamin Butler himself who seemed to realize the full scope of the drama that had unfolded at New Market Heights. Writing to his wife,

A sketch by William Waud of a victorious Ben Butler "bivouacking at the junction of the Varina and New Market Road" on the evening of September 29, 1864, surrounded by captured Rebel flags won during the fighting at Chaffin's Farm. *Harper's Weekly.*

Sarah, at five o'clock that evening, he described the carnage that he had witnessed when he rode over the field earlier that day:

> [Paine's colored troops] *suffered largely and some two hundred of them lay with their backs to the earth and their feet to the fore, with their sable faces made by death a ghastly tawny blue, with their expression of determination, which never dies out of brave men's faces who die instantly in a charge, forming a sad sight, which is burnt on my memory…Poor fellows, they seem to have so little to fight for in this contest, with the weight of prejudice loaded upon them, their lives given to a country which has given them not yet justice, not to say fostering care…But there is one boon they love to fight for, freedom for themselves and their race forever, and "may my right hand forget her cunning" but they shall have that. The man who says the negro will not fight is a coward…His soul is blacker than the faces of these dead negroes, upturned to heaven in solemn protest against him and his prejudices.*

Butler concluded, "I have not been so much moved during this war as I was by that sight."[109]

Chapter 6

FERRO IIS LIBERTAS PERVENIET

While the fierce encounter at New Market Heights was over, the larger battle for Chaffin's Farm would continue throughout the afternoon of the twenty-ninth and on into the next day. After the loss of New Market Heights, the Confederates withdrew to the west, seeking to link up with the protection of the Intermediate Line. While Paine's men were reorganizing and refitting, Birney pushed Terry's and Foster's Divisions up the New Market Road in pursuit. The retreating Rebels in the 3rd Richmond Howitzers, with some of Gary's troopers in support, slowed down the Union advance near Laurel Hill Church, and this delaying action caused doubt and confusion to settle into the advancing Federals. To make matters worse, artillery shells from a Confederate fort to Foster's left started landing amid his soldiers. It turned out that these shells were being fired from Fort Gilmer, and Foster was hesitant about continuing up the New Market Road with such a formidable work in his rear. Thus, he formed his men along the New Market Road, turning to face the destructive fire coming from Gilmer.

It was then roughly three o'clock in the afternoon, and much time had been lost. Foster's first attack on the fort met with heavy casualties, but just like at New Market Heights, a second attempt was made. By this time, Paine's Division had started to arrive, and the poor 5th USCT was ordered to go forward with the second attack, which proved unsuccessful. This would add another 107 casualties to those lost at New Market Heights. A soldier who was there described the volume of fire coming from the fort, stating that his line "disappeared as though an earthquake had swallowed it." Now it was time for the Colored Brigade under William Birney, which had not been

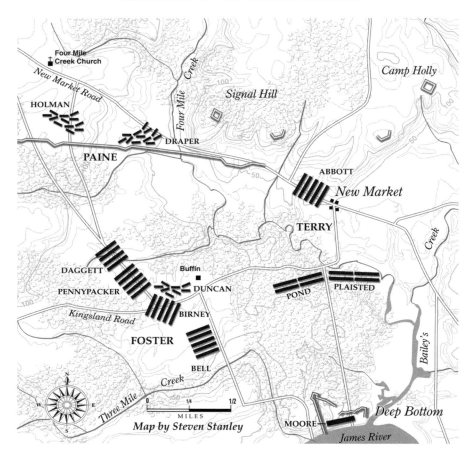

Aftermath of the battle. *Steven Stanley, cartographer.*

in on the action at New Market Heights, to test its mettle. The slaughter that the men faced was just as horrific as that faced by Duncan and Draper's men earlier that day. Birney threw his men in piecemeal, and his units stumbled forward into a murderous fire coming from Confederate troops who were piling into Fort Gilmer for the opportunity to kill a black soldier.[110]

After initial repulses, the elder Birney's staff garbled an order to the 7th USCT, directing it to charge the fort that had defied an entire division earlier in the day with only four companies. When the officer in charge received these orders, he scoffed, "What! Take a fort with a skirmish line? Who ever heard of such a thing? I will try, but it can't be done." And so it was that Companies C, D, G and K went forward, the men knowing full well

Brigadier General Robert S. Foster played a supporting role in the attack on New Market Heights. Later that day, however, his men would be tested as they attempted to take Fort Gilmer (Confederate). *Library of Congress.*

what would happen to them as they stepped out into the open plain, eating artillery fire from the fort as soon as they took the first step. Yet on they went, impervious to the sheets of flame pouring out of Gilmer until they reached the moat that surrounded the fort. Not even Foster's Division had gained this much ground, but with only a skirmish line to begin with, the men were stuck—going back was just as lethal as going forward. After trading a few barbs with the hated black troops occupying the moat of their fort, the Confederates began to light artillery shells and then roll them down on top of the attackers. When the black troops asked for quarter, they were given none; of the 120 men of the 7th USCT who it made into the moat, only 1 survived unscathed—the rest were killed, wounded or, in rare instances, captured. As darkness began to fall, the fighting at Fort Gilmer came to a merciful conclusion.[111]

While the fighting at Fort Gilmer raged, the victors of New Market Heights finally began to push up the New Market Road during the afternoon. As they did so, they came upon a family of slaves who were using the opportunity created by the battle to make their way toward Union lines—and freedom. A reporter from the *Springfield Daily Republican* watched and recounted that the black troops cheered and "gathered about the freedman, and…fairly danced for joy, or cried with delight." The onlooking reporter then commented that "men may have their peculiar views about…the policy of arming blacks; but he who could stand by and see those soldiers…and yet could not share in their joy, and thank God with them that other chains were broken, would have been less than human."[112]

With the fighting for the day finally over, it came time to take account of all that had been lost. For those who were wounded during the battle, they could either be treated by the flying hospital of the 10th Corps or be sent farther back to the base hospital on Jones Neck across from Deep Bottom. The doctors and nurses were able to hear the awful sounds of battle as a steady stream of wounded men came trickling in. Clara Barton wrote in her diary, "I gave out rations all the pm…reports of a great battle & that the 10th corps very near Richmond." One surgeon in the 10th Corps remembered treating the African American soldiers who had fought so hard and won so much on that day. He wrote home in a letter to his wife that "before we went

On the evening of September 29, Clara Barton nursed wounded soldiers at the 10th Corps hospital, set up on Jones Neck across the river from Deep Bottom. *Library of Congress.*

forward to the front, I dressed the wounds of twelve colored men belonging to the 18th Corps. They fought splendidly and I took great satisfaction in doing for them."[113]

The press was quick to pick up on the spectacle that had taken place at New Market Heights. The correspondent for the *New York Herald* wrote on October 4 that the members of Paine's Division "were emphatically the heroes of New Market Heights." Two days earlier, the same paper had reported that "[t]heir charge in the face of the obstacle interposing was one of the grand features of the day's operations. It was made with a vigor and determination that would have done credit to the best organization of white troops in our armies. They never halted or faltered, though their ranks were sadly thinned by the charge." Thomas Morris Chester, a black correspondent for a Philadelphia screed, boasted that the 3rd Division of the 18th Corps

USCTs recuperating at Aiken's Landing, on the north side of the James River, in November 1864. *Library of Congress.*

"has covered itself with glory, and wiped out effectually the imputation against the fighting qualities of the colored troops." Others crowed that "the autocrats of the regular army could croak no longer about the negro soldiers not fighting." Perhaps the most revealing and unlikely admiration came from a Confederate, who wrote after the war that "upon [the] 29th [of] September, Richmond came nearer being captured, and that, too, by negro troops, than it ever did during the whole war."[114]

On October 11, Butler issued an edict praising his soldiers for their bravery in the campaigns of 1864. When it came to New Market Heights, Butler lauded his United States Colored Troops:

> *Of the colored soldiers of the Third Division of the Eighteenth and Tenth Corps and the officers who led them, the general commanding desires to make special mention. In the charge of the enemy's works by the colored division of the Eighteenth Corps at Spring Hill, New Market—better men were never better led, better officers never led better men. With hardly an exception officers of colored troops will be the post of honor in the American armies. The colored soldiers by coolness, steadiness, and determined courage and dash have silenced every cavil of the doubters of their soldierly capacity, and drawn tokens of admiration from their enemies; have brought their late masters even to the consideration of the question whether they will not employ as soldiers the hitherto depised race. Be it so; this war is ended when a musket is in the hands of every ablebodied negro who wishes to use one.*[115]

Butler went on to name specific soldiers who had committed acts of heroism and recommended that many receive promotions and medals to honor their conduct under fire. As a result, fourteen of Paine's black soldiers and two white officers were eventually awarded Medals of Honor.

It appears that Butler felt that his men were slighted by what he thought to be the small number of Medals of Honor that were awarded to them. Thus, being the resourceful Yankee that he was, he decided to have his own medal for gallantry manufactured and awarded to those African American soldiers who distinguished themselves in the Battle of Chaffin's Farm. Not one to skimp on costs, these medals were cast by Tiffany & Company and were modeled after medallions issued by Queen Victoria during the Crimean War. Remarkably, Butler himself footed the bill for the 197 medals that were struck. The medal itself was made of solid silver hung from a red, white and blue ribbon. A wreath reading "Army of the James" was attached to the ribbon, while the front of the medal read, "Distinguished for Courage,

Campaign Before Richmond, 1864." The back of the medal read, "US Colored Troops," and contained a Latin inscription: *Ferro iis libertas perveniet* ("Freedom will be theirs by the sword"). The first medals were issued in May 1865, with more arriving to the 25th Corps later that year. In 1892, Butler proudly said of the medal that bore his name:

> *These I gave with my own hand, save where the recipient was in a distant hospital wounded, and by the commander of the colored corps after it was removed from my command, and I record with pride that in that single action there were so many deserving that it called for a presentation of nearly two hundred. Since the war I have been fully rewarded by seeing the beaming eye of many a colored comrade as he drew his medal from the innermost recesses of its concealment to show me.*

In the twentieth century, there was an effort to have the Butler Medal officially recognized by the Pentagon. Sadly, in 1981, the Department of Defense rejected this movement, stating that it took the position that "a large number of unofficial medals were privately issued to members of the Armed Forces of the United States between 1861 and 1865. The Butler Medal was but one of many in this category."[116]

All things considered, fourteen black soldiers receiving Medals of Honor for one engagement was truly remarkable, considering that only eighteen black Union soldiers were awarded the medal during the entire Civil War. To put things in perspective, the number of medals awarded in the wake of New Market Heights equaled the total number of Medals of Honor issued to black soldiers in the Spanish-American War, World War I and World War II combined. While many view this as a testament to the fortitude of Butler's African American soldiers, some historians have taken issue with this achievement and have questioned the validity of such an accomplishment.

One popular way to analyze the events of September 29, 1864, is to diminish the accomplishments of the black troops and claim that the only reason they were able to take the Confederate trenches along the New Market Line was because the Confederate troops had pulled out to support the Rebels defending Fort Harrison. Richard J. Sommers, in his exceptional *Richmond Redeemed: The Siege at Petersburg*, originated this idea, stating that Butler invented the myth of a great victory at New Market Heights "and trumpeted the event for the rest of his life. Postwar historians of the black troops gladly picked up the theme and modern writers have willingly and uncritically accepted it." Sommers went on to explain that "to go beyond citing physical courage and allege that the blacks won a major tactical victory over the vaunted Texas Brigade belies the historical record... Far from overwhelming a determined foe, Draper in effect charged into a virtually abandoned position and simply chased off a small rear guard from a position already conceded to him." Other sources claim a vast conspiracy to tout the accomplishments of the USCTs initiated by Ben Butler, who used his political prowess to ensure that the medals were handed out. In a 1994 article entitled "A Shower of Stars at New Market Heights," Barry Popchock made the following claim:

> *The Battle of New Market Heights was less than the glorious victory that the self-serving Butler proclaimed. Ord's column, attacking to the west, had captured Fort Harrison on the exterior line. The Confederate defenses were then in danger of cracking wide open. Gregg had pulled his men from the trenches and double-quicked them towards Fort Harrison to shore up the crumbling Confederate line. The black regiments had not swept the enemy off the heights; the Confederates had stopped them as long as they contested the field...Still the occupation of the heights amounted to a small but significant victory, removing a barrier that had stymied the Federal advance for more than three months. The Northerners could see the spires of Richmond, but the view had been dearly bought: more than 900 Union men lay casualties at New Market Heights alone, as against only about 100 Southerners.* [117]

Picking up on Popchock's theme, the author of a recent history of the Hampton Legion scathingly purported that "Ben Butler and his apologists hailed the action at New Market Heights as a great victory for the black troops. It was not that at all; in the second charge the USCTs took the entrenchments from the remnants of the rear guard." Saying that the actions of the Medal of Honor recipients were "nothing extraordinary," the author then went on to soothingly assure the readers that black troops were indeed brave but just poorly led by incompetent white officers. Accordingly, this sad lack of any battlefield victories was so bad that "the Northern press touted New Market Heights as a great victory. It was not that." [118]

Even historian Noah Andre Trudeau latched on to the idea that New Market Heights was a needless bloodbath that no one would have cared about were it not for Butler peddling the story to anyone who crossed his path. Writing in 2008, Trudeau claimed that "for all the heroism and sacrifice, the bitter truth remains that the ultimate justification for the fighting at New Market Heights was neither tactical nor strategic but political." Trudeau went on to state that "black men were ordered into harm's way to prove to the white world that they could fight...[and] the victory won with their blood proved irrelevant to the larger strategic objective of cracking Richmond's defensive ring." He concluded that "the victory won at New Market Heights was needless," even though it did display the fighting prowess of black soldiers once and for all.[119]

So what are we to make of these various historic claims? Did Draper's USCTs simply waltz into a trench line that had been abandoned by the Confederates? Was the New Market Line yielded only when Gregg ordered his men to the defense of nearby Fort Harrison, or were the Rebels driven from their lines and compelled to withdraw, as some accounts claim? And were the sixteen Medals of Honor that were issued to Butler's black soldiers and white officers that day mere tokens thrown at a random handful of survivors so that Butler could puff up their bravery to advance his own political career? In short, was there anything extraordinary about the clash of arms at New Market Heights? Or were fourteen Medals of Honor awarded in a paternalistic effort to vindicate the policy of arming blacks and make something out of nothing?

In order to examine these claims, we must take a look at the disparity between the high regard that modern Americans hold for the Medal of Honor and the accolade as it was in 1864—when it had only existed for two years. Created in July 1862, the Medal of Honor was initially intended to be bestowed "to such noncommissioned officers and privates as shall most distinguish themselves by their gallantry in action, and other soldier-like qualities, during the present insurrection." Legislation was soon passed so that officers could receive the honor as well, and the limitations were dropped so that the award could be won after the war or awarded retroactively. As soon as it was created, however, problems and confusion arose as to how it should be awarded. The wording as to who was eligible to receive the medal was extremely ambiguous and led to much confusion and to the medal being "given out copiously enough to verge on the promiscuous." The most famous instance of this kind of abuse stemmed from the incident in which 864 Medals of Honor were initially awarded to men of the 27th Maine simply for reenlisting.[120]

Confusion and abuse aside, there was never any question that the medal was a badge of valor and should be highly prized. Still, disparity in the ways that the Medal of Honor was sometimes awarded during the Civil War should not be the only criteria used in judging whether the "forgotten

Officers of the 4th USCT in 1865. On the far right is Sergeant Major Christian Fleetwood, proudly wearing his newly issued Medal of Honor. *Library of Congress.*

sixteen" of New Market Heights were worthy of receiving recognition for their deeds. The deeds themselves should speak for their praiseworthiness, and when one looks at the citation for each of the New Market Heights recipients, it is clear that they were very much deserving of veneration.[121]

Six of the Medal of Honor recipients earned their medals by rescuing either the national or regimental flags of their respective units. These flags were important not only for the esprit de corps that they fostered but because they also served a very practical purpose. Amid the smoke and confusion of a battle, individuals who had been separated from their units could look for their colors and rejoin their comrades. "Rally around the colors!" was not just a patriotic recruiting tool—it could mean the difference between victory and defeat. Thus, when Sergeants Charles Veal, Alfred Hilton and Christian Fleetwood of the 4th USCT, as well as Sergeants Alexander Kelly and Thomas Hawkins and Lieutenant Nathan Edgerton of the 6th USCT, all rescued their unit's colors, it was more than a dashing Victorian episode of derring-do. It was an act on which the success or failure of the assault could hinge.[122]

However, the late historian Lee Sturkey purported that rescuing the colors was a "routine" act that was "something that happened time and time again on Civil War battlefields." Because the actions were "routine acts of battlefield courage," Sturkey diminished the celebration of the

First Sergeant Alexander Kelly rescued the national colors of the 6th USCT after Lieutenant Nathan Edgerton was wounded and rallied the men around him. For this action, he received the Medal of Honor. *Library of Congress*.

New Market Heights Medal of Honor recipients as "hoopla…contrived by Butler and his partisans." While it is reasonable to assert that many men who fought for the Union and Confederacy alike risked and, in many instances, lost their lives attempting to save the colors, it does not necessarily follow that the actions of men like Fleetwood were nothing more than "hoopla." Certainly the routineness of a brave act should not be discounted because of how frequently it occurred. Also, the fact that these men exposed themselves in such a way, knowing full well what would happen to them if they fell into enemy hands, seems to give credence to the heroism of their actions. After all, not every soldier who saved a flag during the Civil War ran the risk of being executed after falling into enemy hands simply due to the color of his skin.[123]

Aside from rescuing flags, four black soldiers under Butler's command received Medals of Honor for taking command of their respective companies after their officers had been killed or wounded. This is an act of heroism that

First Sergeant Powhatan Beaty was born a slave near Richmond before moving to Ohio before the Civil War. He joined the 5th USCT and received the Medal of Honor for running back in the face of enemies to retrieve the flag of the 5th before coming back to rally his men. He went on to become a famous Shakespearean actor before dying in 1916. *Library of Congress.*

is arguably more important than saving the regimental colors. Maintaining unit cohesion during battle is a deciding factor, and when Sergeants Powhatan Beaty, James Bronson, Milton Holland, Edward Ratcliff and Robert Pinn took initiative and steadied their men, they literally saved the attack; all four men were in Draper's Brigade, and if their companies had fled, the attack could not have succeeded. Such decisive action by noncommissioned officers is a trait sought by any military force in any epoch of history and is certainly worthy of being honored.[124]

Sergeant James H. Harris of the 38th USCT received his Medal of Honor for "gallantry in the assault" and spent nine months in the hospital after being wounded as Draper's men stormed the works. He was not presented the medal until February 18, 1874. Similarly, Lieutenant William H. Appleton of the 4th USCT was later awarded the medal for "inspiring Union troops by example of steady courage."[125]

An extremely rare image of First Sergeant Milton Holland, 5ᵗʰ USCT, wearing his Medal of Honor. Butler promoted Holland to captain after the battle, but the War Department reversed this promotion solely on the basis of skin color. *Rob Lyon.*

Historian Versalle F. Washington challenged the notion that Draper's men were handed New Market Heights on a silver platter, writing in 1999:

> *Historians have credited the capture of New Market Heights, not to the soldiers' bravery…but to General Gregg's belief that the Federal forces advancing along the Varina Road were a greater threat than the loss of New Market Heights. This is an unlikely interpretation, particularly in light of the rebels' subsequent use of the Texas Brigade and the 25ᵗʰ Virginia Battalion. These forces did not rush to fight the Union forces…General Gregg gave the Confederate infantry the order to retreat once it became clear that they would not be able to hold New Market Heights.*[126]

In the final analysis, the Battle of New Market Heights is worthy of study for multiple reasons. The battle embodies what the Union war effort had come to symbolize by 1864: a struggle to liberate the enslaved and give the

Robert Pinn of the 5th USCT received the Medal of Honor for taking command of his company after all of its officers were either killed or wounded. He was wounded three times and permanently lost the use of his right arm after the attack was over. He went on to attend Oberlin College before dying in 1890. *Library of Congress.*

United States a "new birth of freedom." Emancipation as a policy hinged on the success of the former slaves and free blacks who flocked to the colors after the call went out in 1863. The battles at Fort Wagner and the Crater proved that black soldiers could die nobly, and Fort Pillow provided plenty of indignation. But only clear-cut victories like New Market Heights could convince a war-weary public that the nation's struggle was worth maintaining until final victory had been achieved. In addition to the political and military benefits reaped from the success at New Market Heights, "Beast" Butler and his "Ethiopian cohorts" affirmed the great social experiment that had started when black men were first mustered into the Union army.

As has been shown, the fact that so many United States Colored Troops were awarded Medals of Honor—controversy aside—makes New Market Heights worthy of scrutiny. It is worth noting that these medals were the first ever issued to black men; while most historical works state that Sergeant Major William Carney of the 54th Massachusetts was the first black man to

Born a slave, Sergeant James H. Harris of Company B, 38th USCT, received the Medal of Honor for "gallant conduct" during Draper's assault. It would take Harris nine months to recover from the wounds that he received that day. *Library of Congress.*

receive the Medal of Honor, for his heroism at Battery Wagner in July 1863, they fail to note that he was not awarded the medal until May 1900. The first Medals of Honor awarded to black soldiers during the Civil War took place on April 6, 1865, when the heroes of New Market Heights received their badges of honor.[127]

In October 1864, Major General Benjamin Butler ordered that the words "New Market Heights" be inscribed on the national colors of each black unit that fought there. And 150 years later, it is only fitting that the words should be inscribed on the hearts and minds of those who wish to grapple with the essence of America's most transformative conflict.

Epilogue

THE PERILS OF PRESERVATION

The Battle of Chaffin's Farm represented the Union army's most successful offensive north of the James during the nine-month Richmond-Petersburg Campaign. The day after the capture of New Market Heights, Robert E. Lee himself arrived on the north side with reinforcements to organize a counterattack to retake the ground that had been lost the day before. That Lee would show up in person suggests the importance of these fortifications to the Confederate defense of Richmond. Lee's men attacked in vain, launching three unsuccessful assaults, and the situation in Petersburg, where the Battle of Peebles' Farm was raging, compelled Lee to cut his losses and return to that threatened front. The Confederates tried again on October 7 at the Battle of Darbytown Road and were once again forced to retire—even worse, the Texas Brigade lost General Gregg, who was killed while reconnoitering the area between the Darbytown and New Market Roads.

The last major fighting north of the James took place on October 27, when Butler was ordered to make a demonstration for what would become the Battle of Burgess Mill in Petersburg. This battle, known as Second Fair Oaks, was inconclusive. In January, many of Butler's men were pulled from the lines around Richmond to attack Fort Fisher in Wilmington, North Carolina. This attack would prove to be the undoing of Ben Butler, who was relieved from command of the Army of the James after the First Battle of Fort Fisher ended in failure. However, many of the black troops were sent back to the Virginia front in time to witness the burning of Richmond in early April 1865. The men of the 36th USCT, who had suffered so heavily during Draper's assault on the morning of September 29, were the first foot soldiers to enter the fallen capital on April 3. When the regiment arrived in the city, the soldiers calmly stacked arms while their band played the "Battle Cry of Freedom." Freedom had indeed come by the sword.[128]

After the war was over, the memory of the heroism display at New Market Heights stayed active throughout the latter years of the nineteenth century. In 1866, a book entitled *A Youth's History of the Rebellion* mentioned the battle, claiming that the "Rebels fled from the storming party of blacks, as if the latter were demons." The book also delved into the murky history of prisoners of war being executed, purporting that the Confederates fled because "they appeared to think that no quarter would be shown if they should fall into the hands of their ex-slaves." Just one year later, William Wells Brown published *The Negro in the American Rebellion: His Heroism and His Fidelity* and wrote that "during the battle [of New Market Heights] many instances of unsurpassed bravery were shown by the common soldiers, which proved that these heroic men were fighting for the freedom of their race, and the restoration of a Union that should protect man in his liberty without regard to color." Then, in 1874, Ben Butler—now a congressman—gave a speech in support of his Civil Rights Act. To prove that African Americans were worthy of gaining protections of the citizenship that they were already guaranteed, Butler used New Market Heights as his example. Addressing the House, he bellowed his praise for all to hear:

> *Mr. Speaker, these men have fought for their country...they have shown themselves our equals in battle; as citizens they are kind, quiet, temperate, laborious; they have shown that they know how to exercise the right of suffrage which we have given to them, for they always vote right; they vote the Republican ticket, and all the powers of death and hell cannot persuade them to do otherwise. They show that they knew more than their masters did, for they always knew how to be loyal. They have industry, they have temperance, they have all the good qualities of citizens, they have bravery, they have culture, they have power, they have eloquence. And who shall say that they shall not have what the Constitution gives them—equal rights!*

Unfortunately, Butler was giving his speech at a time when Reconstruction and the power of the Republican Party were both crumbling.[129]

In 1888, George Washington Williams wrote another history of African American service during the Civil War, and his depiction of New Market

Heights borrowed heavily from Butler's speech. At the same time, the veterans themselves were doing everything in their power to keep the memory of the battle alive. Christian Fleetwood published articles and gave speeches, while many of the white officers like Goulding and Duncan addressed the Military Order of the Loyal Legion of the United States, an organization formed in the wake of the Lincoln assassination, touting the brave deeds of the men they once commanded. And as the nineteenth century drew to a close, Joseph T. Wilson—a former USCT himself—did his part to keep the memory of New Market Heights alive. In 1890, he published *The Black Phalanx*, which built on the work of Brown and Williams by chronicling the vital contribution made by African Americans to the Union war effort. Two years later, Wilson ventured into a new arena and published a poem entitled "New Market Heights," which was very brave of him, considering that he was residing in Richmond at the time. The same year that Wilson published his poem, Ben Butler came out with his autobiography, which—all of its historical faults acknowledged—lavished praise yet again on the black soldiers who led the way on September 29, 1864.

As the twentieth century dawned, more and more Civil War veterans were passing away, and the nation was doing its best to heal the dreadful wounds caused by its most lethal conflict. This coincided with the end of Reconstruction and the introduction of Jim Crow policies to the South. In such a volatile atmosphere, talk of the contributions made by black troops during the war had a very limited audience. Still, in 1916, John McMurray, a veteran officer of the 6th USCT, began to publish a series of articles in his local newspaper that would be published under the title of *Recollections of a Colored Troop*. McMurray's memoir was unique in that he relished in calling himself a United States Colored Troop, and he left behind a vivid and engaging account of what he saw—especially at New Market Heights. McMurray only reached a local audience with his book, however. It would be years still before the nation would be reawakened to the Battle of Chaffin's Farm.

The first real tactical study of the battle as a whole was written by Charles J. Calrow. His 1932 work "Battle of Chaffin's Farm, Fort Harrison: A Study" devoted seven of its sixty-five pages to the bloody clash along the New Market Line. However, Calrow's study was once again limited in its scope. In the 1950s and '60s, several general works such as Dudley Taylor Cornish's *The Sable Arm*, William Quarles's *The Negro in the Civil War* and James McPherson's *The Negro's Civil War* all made specific mention of New Market Heights. This paved the way for the doctoral thesis on Grant's Fifth Offensive completed by Richard J. Sommers at Rice University in 1970. Sommers published what was by far the most in-depth study of the entire campaign on both the north and south sides of the James River. Nine years later, a historian with the National Park Service, Ed Bearss, wrote a memo on the Medal of Honor recipients at New Market Heights. While the academic community now had access to a general understanding of the Battle of New Market Heights and the Medal of Honor recipients, that knowledge was not made accessible to the public until Sommers published his doctoral thesis as the classic tactical study *Richmond Redeemed: The Siege at Petersburg* in 1981.

It was not just the academic community that was taking notice of New Market Heights. The October 1975 edition of *Ebony* magazine contained an article as part of its "Great Moments in Black History" series titled "Shootout at Chaffin's Farm: Thirteen Black Soldiers received Medals of Honor for Bravery in Battle in Richmond Suburbs." This cultural piece, written by eminent black historian Lerone Bennett Jr., not only gave the historical details of the Battle of Chaffin's Farm, but it also put the battle into a context of pride and commemoration that the African American community as a whole could celebrate.

Richmond Redeemed opened a door into a previously unexplored facet of the Civil War, and with the success of Sommers's book among Civil War historians and enthusiasts, more scholarship began to emerge that addressed the Army of the James and USCTs. In 1997, Edward G. Longacre released *Army of Amateurs: General Benjamin F. Butler and the Army of the James, 1863–1865*, which is still the only general work on this neglected army. One year later, Noah Andre Trudeau's *Like Men of War: Black Troops in the Civil War, 1862–1865* was released to wide success. At about the same time, Richmond National Battlefield Park historian Michael D. Gorman wrote a small piece titled "Union Perspective of the Battle of New Market Heights" that succinctly summarized the contributions made by African American troops during the battle. The article, along with a host of images, primary sources and maps of the battle, can be found on the park's website.

Another part-time worker for Richmond National Battlefield named Kenneth Brown helped produce a thirty-minute documentary on the Medal of Honor recipients called *The Forgotten Fourteen*—the only documentary of its kind. Unfortunately, the film has gone out of circulation as of the publication of this book.

The twenty-first century has seen much renewed interest in the contributions of United States Colored Troops and the Battle of New Market Heights. In 2004, Dr. Louis H. Manarin produced a history of the Civil War in Henrico County called *Henrico County: Field of Honor* that contained an entire chapter on the Battle of Chaffin's Farm. Manarin's work is lavishly illustrated with detailed maps, rare photographs and original pieces of art, one of which depicts Christian Fleetwood saving the colors during Duncan's assault. In 2006, authors Melvin Claxton and Mark Puls released a book titled *Uncommon Valor: A Story of Race, Patriotism, and Glory during the Civil War*, which told the story of the Medal of Honor recipients with a specific focus on Christian Fleetwood, whose image graces the cover of the book. As the commemoration of the sesquicentennial of the Civil War gets underway in 2011, it seems that public interest is at its peak and that the story of the heroism of Butler's black soldiers at New Market Heights will finally get the attention that it so richly deserves.

In 1865, John Townshend Trowbridge, a well-known Northern writer with abolitionist sentiments, was on a tour of the devastated former states of the Confederacy, taking meticulous notes on the sights that he witnessed and recording many revealing conversations with the locals of each state. In September, he found himself in Richmond and was able to secure an escort who could take him out to see the battle-scarred defenses of the city. This escort was a member of the Army of the James and had participated in the Battle of Chaffin's Farm. When the two riders came up to Fort Gilmer, the unnamed major was overcome with grief. After regaining his composure, the major turned to Trowbridge and said, "I never can look upon this field without emotion. I lost some of my dearest friends in that assault."

Continuing along the New Market Road, the pair then arrived at New Market Heights. Trowbridge recounted his brief visit to the site:

> We next visited New-Market Heights, where Butler's colored regiments formed unflinchingly under fire, and made their gallant charge, wiping out with their own blood the insults that had been heaped upon them by the white troops. "The army saw that charge, and it never insulted a colored soldier after that," said the Major.[130]

Although Trowbridge could not have known it at the time, he was very fortunate to have been able to visit the site—for in a few short years, nature would begin to reclaim the site, and the battle itself would fade from public memory. Indeed, it would not be until the twentieth century that an effort to locate the exact position where Paine's USCTs made their spirited breakthrough would take place, and when it did, it ignited a firestorm of controversy that lingers within the local community to this day.

The 1970s marked the first time that there was a concerted effort to locate the remnants of the New Market Heights battlefield. New development in the eastern portion of Henrico County brought attention to the long-forgotten clashes north of the James River, and as soon as people began to review Civil War–era maps and look at eyewitness accounts to locate the precise point where the USCTs had broken through the New Market Line, controversy began to brew. There was a disagreement over where precisely Butler's black soldiers broke through. One school of thought was that they had pushed through the New Market defenses and captured Camp Holly Hill, well east of Four Mile Creek and Signal Hill. The National Park Service, with legendary historian Ed Bearss leading the charge, disagreed and pointed to the wealth of evidence that indicated that Paine's Division had broken through at a location fronting Signal Hill, due west of where most period maps locate Camp Holly. In 1980, Bearss was quoted as saying that he did not mind being challenged on this matter because "it's part of a game." Bearss said that he loved proving challengers wrong, stating, "I like to destroy them. I'm pretty cocky." Destroy them Bearss did, at least insofar as the amount of historical evidence he gathered to back up his claims. But the controversy would not go away.[131]

In 1981, *Richmond Redeemed* was published, and eight years later the motion picture *Glory* hit theaters across America. That same year, an organization called the Black Military History Institute of America, Inc., lobbied for preservation of the New Market Heights battlefield. The BMHIA sent two letters out on February 16, 1989. The first was to the Department of the Interior:

> *The deeds of these brave and valiant Black fighting men who participated in the struggle for the unity of our nation must no longer be allowed to go unrecognized. To correct this gross oversight, we are requesting that the Department of Interior, under the purview of its charter, take the following action:*
>
> *a. Designate the New Market/Chaffin Farm area as a National Historic Landmark.*
>
> *b. Resurrect the Dept. of Interior's 1979 study to expand Richmond National Battlefield Park to include the New Market Heights Battlefield and Fort Gilmer Extension.*

The same day, a letter went out to then senator John Warner stating, "As we approach the 125th anniversary of the battle, prompt action is necessary if we are to demonstrate that the valiant efforts of these Black soldiers were not in vain."[132]

To cover its bases, the BMHIA also sent a request to the Virginia Department of Conservation and Historic Resources for a state highway marker to be placed near the battlefield.

In the meantime, local landowners began to dispute the claims that the Battle of New Market Heights was fought on their ground. Not only did they dispute the location of the battlefield, they also disputed the date of the battle. They maintained that the battle took place on Signal Hill, north of Route 5 (historic New Market Road), even though a cursory examination of the maps made by the Army of the James in October 1864 clearly shows the battlefield to be south of the road. In retrospect, this seems ludicrous, but these landowners were apparently willing to twist the facts to make sure that the historic battlefield of New Market Heights would not be preserved.

To combat the claims of the local landowners, the BMHIA enlisted the help of Ed Bearss, writing to him on October 4, 1989. However, it appears that the institute was not given a place at the table when meetings and deliberations were held concerning the NHL nomination. Still, the movie *Glory* had been released in December 1989, and it was hoped that the BMHIA could capitalize on the renewed public interest in African American participation in the American Civil War.

Not hearing from Senator Warner's office, Governor Douglas Wilder received a letter on April 6, 1990. That same day, the BMHIA complained that "[t]o date, it is our opinion that efforts to resolve this controversy have not been done in an unbiased and impartial manner."[133]

Finally, in June 1990, a memorandum was released that stated that "the NHL nomination is dead; it will not be pursued any further by the NPS because of near-unanimous owner opposition." The report went on to say that the National Park Service, the County of Henrico and Senator Warner were "all aware that the battle happened to the south of Route 5, not on Signal Hill. Most of the land where the battle really occurred is in the hands of the opponents."[134] And thus ended the battle for making New Market Heights a national historic landmark.

In late 1990, the National Park Service considered other ways to help preserve threatened battlefield land. It proposed to "conserve critical resources and demonstrate the range of potential conservation techniques" for such land.

At New Market Heights, it proposed "a cooperative planning effort for Henrico County's Four Mile Creek Park to conserve battlefield resources and commemorate all those who fought, especially the 14 black Congressional Medal of Honor winners." Once again, such efforts were met with hostility. The vice chairman of the Henrico County Planning Commission at the time was quoted venting, "They're saying, 'We are Yankees, we won the war, now we are going down there and taking the land away from them.' I say to heck with it." Similarly, a Henrico County Board of Supervisors chairman said that "the county should not at any time advocate acquiring private property from any of our Varina land owners for the purpose of battlefield preservation...I certainly understand...the efforts of our national government to preserve our history, but it should not be at the expense of our citizens." A staff report revealed that the opposition was rooted in the fear that the park service's plan would have "serious implications for land available for economic development."[135]

In their landmark publication *Paving Over the Past: A History and Guide to Civil War Battlefield Preservation*, Georgie and Margie Boge noted: "The absence of a preserved area could suggest an irreverent disregard for the valiant efforts of those black columns who advanced on New Market Heights...The present owners continue to contravene plans to commemorate a portion of the battlefield."[136]

On September 29, 1993, a roadside marker was placed on Route 5 to mark the site of the battle. This was accomplished with the assistance of the BMHIA. However, in 1994, the controversy was renewed when the Association for the Preservation of Civil War Sites and the National Park Service joined forces to conduct a survey of battlefield sites around Richmond. Once again, local landowners were irate and vehemently opposed this survey because they thought it was a covert means for a government takeover of their lands. Fears that all of the property designated as important by this survey would result in the loss of land values and bankruptcy were loudly voiced at town hall meetings held throughout Henrico County. In the end, the study was carried out, and no one lost their property. Shortly thereafter, the county began the process of acquiring 177.8 acres of core battlefield property. The ground where Duncan and Draper assaulted was finally safe—or so it seemed.

While the core area of the New Market Heights battlefield was saved, Congressmen Thomas J. Bliley Jr. and Robert C. Scott of Virginia introduced a bill signed into law in 2000 that, among other things, would establish a memorial to the USCTs who died on September 29, 1864.

No funds were appropriated to this project, however. Two years later, the County of Henrico published its *New Market Park Master Plan Report*. It stated that "[t]he County's vision for New Market Park included a new community college for the Varina District" and that an agreement was reached with a local community college to give them "a location in the parklands to create 'a college in the park.'" A New Market Heights visitor center, monument and historic walking trails were included in the plan, but the stark fact remains that a large portion of the battlefield would be erased by heavy construction and the resultant foot and vehicle traffic caused by having a large college present. Indeed, the entry to the park itself would pave over a portion of where Draper's men pierced the New Market Line. To date, no work has been done on this project, and with the current economic state of affairs, it is questionable whether this plan will ever become a reality.[137]

Thankfully, there have been renewed talks about preserving what is left of the battlefield at New Market Heights.

Congressman Bobby Scott has continued his fight to appropriate $10 million for a New Market Heights Memorial and Visitors Center, stating that "[t]he funds will be used for land acquisition, site preparation and toward construction of a memorial and visitor's center at New Market Heights, adjacent to the Richmond National Battlefield Park in Henrico County, Virginia." It remains to be seen what will become of this effort.[138]

In the meantime, the portion of the battlefield where the USCTs made their charge against Confederate defenses remains dormant and undeveloped. Part of this land has been destroyed by a gravel pit that was converted into a large pond before the county purchased the land. The remainder is nearly inaccessible due to the propensity of Four Mile Creek to flood and overflow the dirt road that leads to the site.

Unfortunately, some of the land that was not protected has been lost forever due to a developer who refused to listen to a local preservation group. In a sense, it seems as if the Battle of New Market Heights is still being fought. The Civil War Trust listed New Market Heights as one of America's most endangered battlefields in 2009:

> *Despite New Market Heights' indisputable historic significance, no portion of the battlefield has been protected by any preservation organization, including the National Park Service. Henrico County purchased land within the core of the battlefield several years ago, but it is not open to the public. Only one roadside marker acknowledges the location of the battlefield. Some*

significant portions of the battlefield close to the area where Union troops crossed the James River near Deep Bottom have already been destroyed by a housing development. Additional residential construction underway on the north side of Virginia Route 5, the historic New Market Road, will destroy key Confederate artillery positions. Growing traffic congestion in the region will ultimately necessitate the widening of Route 5, threatening approximately 75 acres of still pristine battlefield land fronting the road.[139]

This long, drawn-out fight to preserve some of America's most hallowed ground has proven to be frustrating and endlessly complicated. While there has been much talk about providing public access to the site and even erecting a monument to the Medal of Honor recipients, all that marks the site is the state roadside marker. If the ongoing commemoration of the sesquicentennial of the American Civil War is to have any truly lasting impact, the preservation and interpretation of endangered sites like the New Market Heights battlefield must top any list of priorities.

Until this situation changes, Joseph T. Wilson's poetic lament first published in 1892 will remain a tragic reality:

No marble shaft or granate pile mark the spot
Where they fell—their bones lay harvested from sun-rot,
In the Nation's cities of the dead. Hannibal led
No braver than they through Alpine snow, nor wed
To freedom were Greece's phalanx more, who o'er gory
  clay
Followed Butler to New Market heights that day.[140]

NOTES

PREFACE

1. Blackett, *Thomas Morris Chester*, 142.
2. Carter, "Fourteen Months' Service with Colored Troops," 179.
3. Williams claimed that "the Union flag was planted on Fort Harrison by Negro troops," which is a severe distortion, considering that no black troops were involved in the initial assaults at Fort Harrison on the morning of September 29, 1864. Williams, *History of Negro Troops*, 252.
4. Butler, *Butler's Book*, 733.

CHAPTER 1

5. McMurray, *Recollections of a Colored Troop*, 52.
6. Grant, *Personal Memoirs of U.S. Grant*, 365–67.
7. Quoted in Grant, *Personal Memoirs of U.S. Grant*, 369.
8. Fox, *Regimental Losses in the American Civil War*, 561.
9. Nevins, Thomas and Pressly, *Diary of George Templeton Strong*, 467, 474.
10. Quoted in Fehrenbacher and Fehrenbacher, *Recollected Words of Abraham Lincoln*, 196.
11. Sommers, *Richmond Redeemed*, 4.
12. Varon, *Southern Lady, Yankee Spy*, 107, 253–56.
13. Winkler, *Stealing Secrets*, 721.

14. Jones, *Personal Reminiscences, Anecdotes, and Letters*, 40.

15. Rafuse, *Robert E. Lee and the Fall of the Confederacy*, 179.

16. Moore, *Story of a Cannoneer Under Stonewall Jackson*, 263.

17. Quoted in Trudeau, "A Mere Question of Time" in Gallagher, *Lee the Soldier*, 545.

18. Wert, *From Winchester to Cedar Creek*, 33.

19. General Orders No. 214, February 24, 1864.

20. Pfanz, *Richard S. Ewell*, 403.

21. Hess, *In the Trenches at Petersburg*, 10; Sommers, *Richmond Redeemed*, 15; Jones, *Campbell Brown's Civil War*, 269.

22. Sommers, *Richmond Redeemed*, 34; Simpson, *Hood's Texas Brigade*, 195.

CHAPTER 2

23. Longacre, "Black Troops in the Army of the James," 1. Longacre states that 40 percent of the Army of the James consisted of USCTs.

24. Trefousse, *Ben Butler*, 20, 24–26; Nolan, *Benjamin Franklin Butler*, 41.

25. Nolan, *Benjamin Franklin Butler*, 34; Trefousse, *Ben Butler*, 58.

26. Trefousse, *Ben Butler*, 68.

27. Quoted in Cornish, *Sable Arm*, 24.

28. Cornish, *Sable Arm*, 58–67; Berlin, Reidy and Rowland, *Freedom's Soldiers*, 9. For more on this controversy, see "Benjamin Butler's Enlistment of Black Troops in New Orleans in 1862" in Westwood, *Black Troops, White Commanders and Freedmen*, 37–54; Longacre, *Army of Amateurs*, 8.

29. Terry in Carleton, *Report of the Proceedings*, 34; Sommers, *Richmond Redeemed*, 18.

30. Longacre, *Army of Amateurs*, 27.

31. Quoted in Blight, *Frederick Douglass' Civil War*, 163.

32. General Order No. 143, May 22, 1863; Orders and Circulars, 1797–1910; Records of the Adjutant General's Office, 1780s–1917, National Archives, RG 94.

33. Johnson and Buel, "Opposing Forces at the Beginning of Grant's Campaign," 181–82; Butler, *Butler's Book*, 672; Page, *Letters of a War Correspondent*, 242.

34. Pope, *Paine Ancestry*, 239–40, 256–58; Sommers, *Richmond Redeemed*, 31.

35. Biographical Sketch, Personal Papers of John Holman, State Historical Society of Missouri; Gibbs, *Black, Copper & Bright*, 49–50, 2.

36. Gibbs, *Black, Copper & Bright*, 27, 41, 57, 80; Bates, *History of Pennsylvania Volunteers*, vol. 5, 991; Reid, *Freedom for Themselves*, 52, 56, 163, 166.

37. Draper, *Drapers in America*, 208–10; Reid, *Freedom for Themselves*, 43–44.

38. Washington, *Eagles on Their Buttons*, 1, 12, 14, 30, 34, 37, 42, 47; Reid, *Freedom for Themselves*, 42, 44, 46, 49, 131, 134, 137.

39. Buffum, *Memorial of the Great Rebellion*, 43; Longacre, *Regiment of Slaves*, 22–23.

40. Longacre, *Regiment of Slaves*, x; Paradis, *Strike the Blow for Freedom*, 13, 40–41, 43–47, 53, 61.

41. Ofele, *German-Speaking Officers*, 179.

42. Quoted in Berlin, Reidy and Rowland, *Freedom*, 572.

43. *The War of the Rebellion: A Compilation of the Official Records of the Union and Confederate Armies*, ser. II, vol. 5, 797 (hereafter cited as *OR*).

44. Polley, *Soldier's Letter*, 249.

CHAPTER 3

45. For more on the First Battle of Deep Bottom, see Manarin, *Henrico County*, vol. 2, 415–36.

46. *OR*, ser. I, vol. 42, pt. 1, 242, 661.

47. Butler, *Butler's Book*, 721; *Atlanta Journal*, "One of 'Old Rock's' Brigade," Saturday evening, April 19, 1902.

48. Butler, *Butler's Book*, 721–22; Marshall, *Private and Official Correspondence*, vol. 5, 168.

49. Marshall, *Private and Official Correspondence*, vol. 5, 172–73.

50. *OR*, ser. I, vol. 42, pt. 2, 1,082.

51. Ibid., 1,083.

52. Ibid., 1,087.

53. *Fraser's Magazine for Town and Country*, "A Visit to General Butler," 435; Marshall, *Private and Official Correspondence*, 174.

54. McMurray, *Recollections of a Colored Troop*, 50; National Humanities Center Resource Toolbox, "Diary of Sergeant Major Christian Fleetwood," 4.

55. Davis, *Life of David Bell Birney*, 257.

56. Hyde, *History of the One Hundred and Twelfth Regiment*, 101.

57. Ibid., 102; *OR*, ser. I, vol. 42, pt. 1, 760.

58. Committee of the Regimental Association, *Story of One Regiment*, 270; Stowits, *History of the One Hundredth Regiment*, 305.

59. Longacre, *From Antietam to Fort Fisher*, 208–9.
60. Sommers, *Richmond Redeemed*, 27; quoted in Trudeau, *Like Men of War*, 284; *OR*, ser. I, vol. 42, pt. 1, 764, 760, 767; Hyde, *History of the One Hundred and Twelfth Regiment*, 102; Roe, *Twenty-Fourth Regiment Massachusetts Volunteers*, 360; Longacre, *From Antietam to Fort Fisher*, 209.
61. Edward L. Cook to sister in Wixson, *Echoes from the Boys of Company "H,"* 378.
62. National Humanities Center Resource Toolbox, "Diary of Sergeant Major Christian Fleetwood," 4.

CHAPTER 4

63. *Fraser's Magazine for Town and Country*, "A Visit to General Butler," 438.
64. Winkler, *Confederate Capital*, 192; Edward R. Crockett Diary, Richmond National Battlefield Park; Mulholland, *Military Order Congress Medal of Honor*, 516–17.
65. Trumball, *Knightly Soldier*, 297; Dickey, *History of the Eighty-fifth Regiment*, 354.
66. *OR*, ser. I, vol. 42, pt. 1, 819.
67. Ibid., 760.
68. Sommers, *Richmond Redeemed*, 33.
69. Pope, *Paine Ancestry*, 258; Record of Events, Muster Rolls of 4th and 6th U.S. Colored Troops, National Archives, RG 94; Sommers, *Richmond Redeemed*, 582, n22.
70. *Fraser's Magazine for Town and Country*, "A Visit to General Butler," 435.
71. Goulding, "Colored Troops in the War of the Rebellion," 149.
72. Mulholland, *Military Order Congress Medal of Honor*, 516.
73. McMurray, *Recollections of a Colored Troop*, 51–52.
74. Butler quoted in *American Annual Cyclopaedia*, vol. 14, 212.
75. Augustus Boernstein, letter, October 4, 1864, quoted in *Rail Splitter*.
76. Polley, *Soldier's Letter*, 259; Waring, "Diary of William G. Hinson," 111; Thomas C. McCarty Diary, September/October 1864, Eugene C. Barker Texas History Center, University of Texas at Austin.
77. Polley, *Hood's Texas Brigade*, 253; quoted in Furness, "Negro as a Soldier," 483; May, "Fight at Fort Gilmer," 588.
78. Hanks, *History of Captain B.F. Benton's Company*, 36.
79. Hamilton, *History of Company M*, 61–62; Hanks, *History of Captain B.F. Benton's Company*, 37; Pope, *Paine Ancestry*, 258.

80. Mulholland, *Military Order Congress Medal of Honor*, 517.

81. McMurray, *Recollections of a Colored Troop*, 51.

82. Goulding, "Colored Troops in the War of the Rebellion," 150.

83. Ritter, "Congressional Medal of Honor Winners," 135–36.

84. Christian Fleetwood to Septimus Tustin, March 2, 1870, National Archives, RG 94, Thomas R. Hawkins Pension File; Kelly questionnaire, Burton Historical Collection, Detroit Public Library, Frederick Keydell MSS Collection.

85. Yeary, *Reminiscences of the Boys in Gray*, 62; quoted in Trudeau, *Like Men of War*, 290; Goulding, "Colored Troops in the War of the Rebellion," 150; McMurray, *Recollections of a Colored Troop*, 54.

86. *OR*, ser. I, vol. 42, pt. 1, 817.

87. *OR*, ser. I, vol. 42, pt. 1, 702, 708.

88. Elliott F. Grabill to Anna, September 30, 1864, Oberlin College, RG 30/43, Papers of Elliott Grabill.

89. Samuel Duncan to Julia, October 22, 1864, Duncan-Jones Papers, New Hampshire Historical Society.

90. *OR*, ser. I, vol. 42, pt. 1, 136.

Chapter 5

91. Burkhart, *Double Duty in the Civil War*, 122; Newton, *Out of the Briars*, 55.

92. *Fraser's Magazine for Town and Country*, "A Visit to General Butler," 438–39.

93. Dameron, *Benning's Brigade*, vol. 1, 81; Jones, "Texas and Arkansas at Fort Harrison," 24; May, "Fight at Fort Gilmer," 588; Krick, *Civil War Weather in Virginia*, 139; Manarin, *Henrico County*, vol. 2, 620.

94. *OR*, ser. I, vol. 42, pt. 1, 819; Blackett, *Thomas Morris Chester*, 150.

95. *OR*, ser. I, vol. 42, pt. 1, 819.

96. Ibid.

97. Thomas C. McCarty Diary, September/October 1864; Edward R. Crockett Diary, Richmond National Battlefield; Austin, *Georgia Boys with "Stonewall" Jackson*, 70.

98. Synnestvedt, "Joseph Scroggs"; Draper, *Drapers in America*, 211; Sommers, *Richmond Redeemed*, 36–37.

99. *OR*, ser. I, vol. 42, pt. 1, 708, 712, 719.

100. Ibid., 702, 708, 820.

101. Synnestvedt, "Joseph Scroggs"; Elliot Grabill to Anna, September 30, 1864, GR 30/43, Papers of Elliott Grabill.

102. *OR*, ser. I, vol. 42, pt. 1, 819–20; Carter, "Fourteen Months' Service with Colored Troops," 171; Perdue Jr., Barden and Phillips, *Weevils in the Wheat*, 103.

103. White, *Contributions to a History of the Richmond Howitzer Battalion*, 273–74; *OR*, ser. I, vol. 42, pt.1, 817–18.

104. Crosland, *Reminiscences of the Sixties*, 34; Waring, "Diary of William G. Hinson," 111; Moore, *Story of a Cannoneer Under Stonewall Jackson*, 263.

105. *OR*, ser. I, vol. 42, pt. 1, 760, 1,109; *Fraser's Magazine for Town and Country*, "A Visit to General Butler," 439.

106. Pickens, "Fort Harrison," 484; Thomas C. McCarty Diary, September/October 1864; Winkler, *Confederate Capital*, 194; Hamilton, *History of Company M*, 61–62.

107. Goulding, "Colored Troops in the War of the Rebellion," 150.

108. Longacre, *From Antietam to Fort Fisher*, 209; Hyde, *History of the One Hundred and Twelfth Regiment*, 103; Stowits, *History of the One Hundredth Regiment*, 306.

109. Marshall, *Private and Official Correspondence*, 191–92.

Chapter 6

110. Longacre, *From Antietam to Fort Fisher*, 211; Edward Porter Alexander said that "many of the Texans & Georgians…came running into the fort & asking for 'a chance to shoot a nigger'" in Gallagher, *Fighting for the Confederacy*, 478.

111. *OR*, ser. I, vol. 42, pt. 1, 724; Sherman, "Negro as a Soldier," 21.

112. Quoted in Trudeau, *Like Men of War*, 293–94.

113. Quoted in Oates, *Woman of Valor*, 270; Chaplin William L. Hyde to Wife, October 1, 1864, at http://www.12thnyvi.com/page4.html.

114. *New York Herald*, "The Colored Troops the Heroes of New Market Heights," October 4, 1864; *New York Herald*, "Movement of the Tenth Corps," October 2, 1864; Blackett, *Thomas Morris Chester*, 140; Wilson, *Black Phalanx*, 435; Johnston, "Attack on Fort Gilmer," 438.

115. *OR*, ser. I, vol. 42, pt. 3, 169.

116. Gladstone, *United States Colored Troops*, 70; Butler, *Butler's Book*, 742–43; Trudeau, "Needless Valor," 65.

117. Sommers, *Richmond Redeemed*, 38; Popchock, "Shower of Stars at New Market Heights," 39.

118. Sturkey, *Hampton Legion*, 89, 553 n175, 90.

119. Trudeau, "Needless Valor," 57, 65.

120. For more on this, see Pullen, *Shower of Stars*.

121. Mikaelian and Wallace, *Medal of Honor*, xviii.

122. *OR*, ser. I, vol. 42, pt. 3, 169.

123. Sturkey, *Hampton Legion*, 553–54 n175.

124. *OR*, ser. I, vol. 42, pt. 3, 168.

125. U.S. Congress, Senate documents, 66th Cong., 1st sess., May 19–November 19, 1919, vol. 14, 362.

126. Washington, *Eagles on Their Buttons*, 56–57.

127. See http://sablearm.blogspot.com/2011/02/how-many-black-union-soldiers-won-medal.html.

Epilogue

128. Reid, *Freedom for Themselves*, 150–51.

129. Thayer, *Youth's History of the Rebellion*, 174; Brown, *Negro in the American Rebellion*, 378–79; *American Annual Cyclopaedia*, 212.

130. Trowbridge, *Picture of the Desolated States and the Work of Restoration*, 200.

131. *Richmond Times Dispatch*, "Neither Side Willing to Retreat in War," July 18, 1980.

132. William A. De Shields to Department of the Interior, February 16, 1989; William A. De Shields to Senator John W. Warner, February 16, 1989.

133. William A. De Shields to Senator John W. Warner, April 6, 1990.

134. John S. Salmon, Historian, Memorandum to Bob Carter, June 20, 1990.

135. City of Richmond, "Conserving Richmond's Battlefields," 51; Kelly, "Henrico Fires Warning Shots."

136. Boge and Boge, *Paving Over the Past*, 72–73.

137. County of Henrico, *New Market Park Master Plan Report*, 4.

138. Congress Bobby Scott website, "Project Requests Submitted by Congressman Scott."

139. Civil War Preservation Trust, *History Under Siege 2009*, 6.

140. Wilson, *Voice of a New Race*, 43.

BIBLIOGRAPHY

NEWSPAPERS

Atlanta Journal.
New York Herald.
Richmond Times Dispatch.

MANUSCRIPT COLLECTIONS

Archives, Oberlin College, Oberlin, Ohio
    RG 30/43, Papers of Elliott Grabill.
    RG 30/32, Papers of Giles Waldo and Mary E. Burton Shurtleff.
Archives, Richmond National Battlefield Park, Richmond, Virginia
    Edward R. Crockett Diary.
Archives, State Historical Society of Missouri, Columbia, Missouri
    Personal Papers of John Holman.
Burton Historical Collection, Detroit Public Library, Detroit, Michigan
    Frederick Keydell Manuscript Collection.
Eugene C. Barker Texas History Center, University of Texas at Austin, Austin, Texas
    Thomas C. McCarty Diary, September/October 1864.
Manuscript Collection, New Hampshire Historical Society, Concord, New Hampshire
    Duncan-Jones Papers.

National Archives and Records Administration, Washington, D.C.
  RG 94, Orders and Circulars, 1797–1910; Records of the Adjutant General's Office, 1780s–1917.
  RG 94, Record of Events, Muster Rolls of 4th and 6th U.S. Colored Troops.
  RG 94, Thomas R. Hawkins Pension File.

PUBLISHED PRIMARY SOURCES

Articles

Carter, Solon A. "Fourteen Months' Service with Colored Troops." *Civil War Papers, Read Before the Commandery of the State of Massachusetts, Military Order of the Loyal Legion of the United States.* Vol. 1. Boston: The Commandery of the State of Massachusetts Military Order of the Loyal Legion of the United States, 1900, 154–79.

Fraser's Magazine for Town and Country 71, no. 424. "A Visit to General Butler and the Army of the James, Part the First" (April 1865): 434–48.

Furness, William Eliot. "The Negro as a Soldier." *Military Essays and Recollections: Papers Read Before the Commandery of the State of Illinois, Military Order of the Loyal Legion of the United States.* Vol. 2. Chicago, IL: A.C. McClurg and Company, 1894, 457–87.

Goulding, J.H. "The Colored Troops in the War of the Rebellion." *Proceedings of the Reunion Society of Vermont Officers.* Vol. 2. *1886–1905.* Burlington, VT: Free Press Printing Company, 1906, 137–54.

Johnson, Robert Underwood, and Clarence Clough Buel, eds. "The Opposing Forces at the Beginning of Grant's Campaign Against Richmond." *Battles and Leaders of the Civil War.* Vol. 4. New York: Century Company, 1888, 179–84.

Johnston, Charles. "Attack on Fort Gilmer, September 29th, 1864." *Southern Historical Society Papers* 1 (January–June, 1876): 438–42.

Jones, A.C. "Texas and Arkansas at Fort Harrison." *Confederate Veteran* 25 (1917): 24–27.

May, T.J. "The Fight at Fort Gilmer." *Confederate Veteran* 12 (1904): 588.

National Humanities Center Resource Toolbox. "The Making of African American Identity: Vol. 1, 1500–1865: Diary of Sergeant Major Christian Fleetwood," excerpts. http://nationalhumanitiescenter.org/pds/index.htm.

Pickens, J.D. "Fort Harrison." *Confederate Veteran* 21 (1913): 483–85.

Sherman, George R. "The Negro as a Soldier." *Personal Narratives of Events in the War of the Rebellion, Being Papers Read Before the Rhode Island Soldiers and Sailors Historical Society.* Seventh series, no. 7. Providence, RI: Snow & Farnham Co., Printers, 1913, 1–34.

Synnestvedt, Sig, ed. "Joseph Scroggs: Observations from His Diary about the 1864 Petersburg Campaign." *Civil War Times Illustrated*, December 1972.

Waring, Joseph I., ed. "The Diary of William G. Hinson during the War of Secession, Part II (Continued from January, 1974)." *South Carolina Historical Magazine* 75, no. 2 (April 1974): 14–23.

Books

The American Annual Cyclopaedia and Register of Important Events of the Year 1874. Vol. 14. New York: D. Appleton and Company, 1875.

Berlin, Ira, Joseph P. Reidy and Leslie S. Rowland, eds. *Freedom: A Documentary History of Emancipation 1861–1867.* Series II. *The Black Military Experience.* Cambridge, UK: Cambridge University Press, 1982.

———. *Freedom's Soldiers: The Black Military Experience in the Civil War.* Cambridge, UK: Cambridge University Press, 1998.

Blackett, R.J.M., ed. *Thomas Morris Chester, Black Civil War Correspondent: His Dispatches from the Virginia Front.* Baton Rouge: Louisiana State University, 1989.

Burkhart, George S., ed. *Double Duty in the Civil War: The Letters of Sailor and Soldier Edward W. Bacon.* Carbondale: Southern Illinois University Press, 2009.

Butler, Benjamin F. *Butler's Book: A Review of His Legal, Political, and Military Career.* Boston, MA: A.M. Thayer & Company, 1892.

Carleton, Charles A., ed. *Report of the Proceedings of the Society of the Army of the James at the First Triennial Reunion, Held in Boston, Massachusetts, September 2d, 1868.* New York: Carleton, Publisher, Madison Square, 1869.

Civil War Preservation Trust. *History Under Siege 2009: A Guide to America's Most Endangered Civil War Battlefields.* www.civilwar.org/history-under-siege/2009-history-under-siege.pdf.

County of Henrico. *New Market Park Master Plan Report.* Submitted by Timmons, February 22, 2002.

Crosland, Charles. *Reminiscences of the Sixties.* Columbia, SC: State Company, 1910.

Fehrenbacher, Don Edward, and Virginia Fehrenbacher, eds. *Recollected Words of Abraham Lincoln*. Palo Alto, CA: Stanford University Press, 1996.

Gallagher, Gary W., ed. *Fighting for the Confederacy: The Personal Recollections of General Edward Porter Alexander*. Chapel Hill: University of North Carolina Press, 1989.

Grant, Ulysses S. *Personal Memoirs of U.S. Grant*. Vol. 2. New York: Charles L. Webster & Company, 1885.

Jones, J. William. *Personal Reminiscences, Anecdotes, and Letters of Gen. Robert E. Lee*. New York: D. Appleton and Company, 1875.

Jones, Terry L., ed. *Campbell Brown's Civil War: With Ewell and the Army of Northern Virginia*. Baton Rouge: Louisiana State University Press, 2001.

Longacre, Edward G., ed. *From Antietam to Fort Fisher: The Civil War Letters of Edward King Wightman, 1862–1865*. Cranbury, NJ: Associated University Press, 1985.

Marshall, Jessie Ames, ed. *Private and Official Correspondence of Gen. Benjamin F. Butler*. Vol. 5. Norwood, MA: Plimpton Press, 1917.

McMurray, John. *Recollections of a Colored Troop*. Brookville, PA: McMurray Company, 1994, reprint edition.

Moore, Edward A. *The Story of a Cannoneer Under Stonewall Jackson*. New York: Neale Publishing Company, 1907.

Nevins, Allan, Milton P. Thomas and Thomas Pressly, eds. *The Diary of George Templeton Strong* [abridged]. Seattle: University of Washington Press, n.d.

Newton, A.H. *Out of the Briars: An Autobiography and Sketch of the Twenty-ninth Regiment Connecticut Volunteers*. Miami, FL: Mnemosyne Publishing Company, Inc., 1969.

Page, Charles A. *Letters of a War Correspondent*. Boston, MA: L.C. Page and Company, 1899.

Perdue, Charles L., Jr., Thomas E. Barden and Robert K. Phillips, eds. *Weevils in the Wheat: Interviews with Virginia Ex-Slaves*. Charlottesville: University Press of Virginia, 1991.

Polley, Joseph. *A Soldier's Letters to Charming Nellie*. New York: Neale Publishing Company, 1908.

Trowbridge, John T. *A Picture of the Desolated States and the Work of Restoration, 1865–1868*. Hartford, CT: L. Stebbins, 1868.

U.S. Congress. Senate documents. 66th Cong., 1st sess., May 19–November 19, 1919. Vol. 14. Washington, D.C.: Government Printing Office, 1919.

The War of the Rebellion: A Compilation of the Official Records of the Union and Confederate Armies. 128 vols., 3 series. Washington, D.C.: United States Government Printing Office, 1889.

White, William S. *Contributions to a History of the Richmond Howitzer Battalion, Pamphlet No. 2: A Diary of the War or What I Saw*. Richmond, VA: Carlton McCarthy & Company, 1883.

Winkler, A.V. *The Confederate Capital and Hood's Texas Brigade*. Austin, TX: Eugene Von Boeckmann, 1894.

Wixson, Neal E., ed. *Echoes from the Boys of Company "H."* New York: iUniverse, Inc., 2008.

Yeary, Mamie, ed. *Reminiscences of the Boys in Gray, 1861–1865*. Dayton, OH: Morningside, 1986.

Website

Congressman Bobby Scott website. "Project Requests Submitted by Congressman Scott for the FY 2011 Appropriations Process." http://www.bobbyscott.house.gov/index.php?option=com_content&view=article&id=480&Itemid=123.

SECONDARY SOURCES

Articles

Boernstein, Augustus, letter, October 4, 1864. In *The Rail Splitter: A Journal for the Lincoln Collector*, September 28, 2006.

Kelly, Deborah. "Henrico Fires Warning Shots at Park Proposal." *Richmond Times Dispatch*, Friday, April 12, 1991.

Longacre, Edward G. "Black Troops in the Army of the James, 1863–65." *Military Affairs* 45, no. 1 (1981): 1–8.

Popchock, Barry. "A Shower of Stars at New Market Heights." *Civil War: The Magazine of the Civil War Society* 46 (August 1994): 30–31, 34–39.

Ritter, E. Jay. "Congressional Medal of Honor Winners." *Negro History Bulletin* 23 (1960): 135–36.

Trudeau, Noah Andre. "Needless Valor." *MHQ: The Quarterly Journal of Military History* 21, no. 1 (Autumn 2008): 56–65.

Books

Austin, Aurelia, ed. *Georgia Boys with "Stonewall" Jackson: James Thomas Thompson and the Walton Infantry*. Athens: University of Georgia Press, 1967.

Bates, Samuel P. *History of Pennsylvania Volunteers, 1861–5.* Vol. 5. Harrisburg, PA: B. Singerly, State Printer, 1871.

Blight, David W. *Frederick Douglass' Civil War: Keeping Faith in Jubilee.* Baton Rouge: Louisiana State University Press, 1989.

Boge, Georgie, and Margie H. Boge. *Paving Over the Past: A History and Guide to Civil War Battlefield Preservation.* Washington, D.C.: Inland Press, 1993.

Buffum, Francis H. *A Memorial of the Great Rebellion: Being a History of the Fourteenth New Hampshire Volunteers, Covering Its Three Years of Service, with Original Sketches of Army Life, 1862–1865.* Boston, MA: Franklin Press: Rand, Avery & Company, 1882.

City of Richmond. "Conserving Richmond's Battlefields: A Collaborative Project Among Concerned Citizens; Local Planning, Preservation and Promotion Groups; Chesterfield, Hanover and Henrico Counties; The City of Richmond; The Commonwealth of Virginia; and the National Park Service." Draft. Richmond, VA: City of Richmond, October 1990.

Committee of the Regimental Association, comp. *The Story of One Regiment: The Eleventh Maine Infantry in the War of the Rebellion.* New York: Press of J.J. Little & Company, 1906.

Cornish, Dudley Taylor. *The Sable Arm: Negro Troops in the Union Army, 1861–1865.* New York: W.W. Norton & Company, Inc., 1956.

Dameron, J. David. *Benning's Brigade.* Vol. 1. *A History and Roster of the Fifteenth Georgia.* Westminster, MD: Heritage Books, Inc., 1997.

Davis, Oliver Wilson. *Life of David Bell Birney, Major-General United States Volunteers.* Philadelphia, PA: King & Baird, 1867.

Dickey, Luther S. *History of the Eighty-fifth Regiment of Pennsylvania Volunteer Infantry, 1861–1865.* New York: J.C. and W.E. Powers, 1915.

Draper, Thomas Waln-Morgan, ed. *The Drapers in America: Being a History and Genealogy of Those of That Name and Connection.* New York: John Polhemus Printing Company, 1892.

Fox, William F., Lieutenant Colonel, USV. *Regimental Losses in the American Civil War, 1861–1865.* Albany, NY: Albany Publishing Company, 1889.

Gallagher, Gary W., ed. *Lee the Soldier.* Lincoln: University of Nebraska Press, 1996.

Gibbs, C.R. *Black, Copper & Bright: The District of Columbia's Black Civil War Regiment.* Silver Spring, MD: Three Dimensional Publishing, 2002.

Gladstone, William A. *United States Colored Troops, 1863–1867.* Gettysburg, PA: Thomas Publications, 1990.

Hamilton, D.H. *History of Company M, First Texas Volunteer Infantry, Hood's Brigade, Longstreet's Corps, Army of the Confederate States of America*. Waco, TX: W.M. Morrison, 1962.

Hanks, O.T. *History of Captain B.F. Benton's Company, Hood's Texas Brigade, 1861–1865*. Austin, TX: Morrison Books, 1984.

Hess, Earl J. *In the Trenches at Petersburg: Field Fortifications & Confederate Defeat*. Chapel Hill: University of North Carolina Press, 2009.

Hyde, William L. *History of the One Hundred and Twelfth Regiment N.Y. Volunteers*. Fredonia, NY: W. McKinstry & Company Publishers, 1866.

Krick, Robert K. *Civil War Weather in Virginia*. Tuscaloosa: University of Alabama Press, 2007.

Longacre, Edward G. *Army of Amateurs: General Benjamin F. Butler and the Army of the James, 1863–1865*. Mechanicsburg, PA: Stackpole Books, 1997.

———. *A Regiment of Slaves: The 4th United States Colored Infantry, 1863–1866*. Mechanicsburg, PA: Stackpole Books, 2003.

Mikaelian, Allen, and Mike Wallace. *Medal of Honor: Profiles of America's Military Heroes from the Civil War to the Present*. New York: Hyperion Books, 2002.

Mulholland, St. Clair Augustin. *Military Order Congress Medal of Honor Legion of the United States*. Philadelphia, PA: Town Printing, 1905.

Nolan, Dick. *Benjamin Franklin Butler: The Damndest Yankee*. Novato, CA: Presidio Press, 1991.

Oates, Stephen B. *A Woman of Valor: Clara Barton and the Civil War*. New York: Free Press, 1994.

Ofele, Martin. *German-Speaking Officers in the U.S. Colored Troops, 1863–1867*. Gainesville: University Press of Florida, 2004.

Paradis, James M. *Strike the Blow for Freedom: The 6th United States Colored Infantry in the Civil War*. Shippensburg, PA: White Mane Books, 2000.

Pfanz, Donald C. *Richard S. Ewell: A Soldier's Life*. Chapel Hill: University of North Carolina Press, 1998.

Polley, Joseph. *Hood's Texas Brigade: Its Marches, Its Battles, Its Achievements*. New York: Neale Publishing Company, 1910.

Pope, Charles H., ed. *Paine Ancestry: The Family of Robert Treat Paine, Signer of the Declaration of Independence, Including Maternal Lines*. Boston, MA: Press of David Clapp & Son, 1912.

Pullen, John J. *A Shower of Stars: The Medal of Honor and the 27th Maine*. Mechanicsburg, PA: Stackpole Books, 1966.

Rafuse, Ethan S. *Robert E. Lee and the Fall of the Confederacy, 1863–1865*. Lanham, MD: Rowman & Littlefield Publishers, Inc., 2008.

Reid, Richard M. *Freedom for Themselves: North Carolina's Black Soldiers in the Civil War Era*. Chapel Hill: University of North Carolina Press, 2008.

Roe, Alfred S. *The Twenty-Fourth Regiment Massachusetts Volunteers 1861–1866*. Worcester, MA: Twenty-Fourth Veteran Association, 1907.

Simpson, Harold B. *Hood's Texas Brigade: Lee's Grenadier Guard*. Waco, TX: Texican Press, 1970.

Stowits, George H. *History of the One Hundredth Regiment of New York State Volunteers*. Buffalo, NY: Printing House of Matthews & Warren, 1870.

Sturkey, O. Lee. *The Hampton Legion*. Wilmington, NC: Broadfoot Publishing Company, 2008.

Thayer, William H. *A Youth's History of the Rebellion, From the Massacre at Fort Pillow to the End*. Boston, MA: Walker, Fuller and Company, 1866.

Trefousse, Hans Louis. *Ben Butler: The South Called Him BEAST!* New York: Twayne Publishers, 1957.

Trumball, Henry Clay. *The Knightly Soldier: A Biography of Major Henry Ward Camp, Tenth Connecticut Volunteers*. Boston, MA: Nichols & Noyes, 1865.

Varon, Elizabeth R. *Southern Lady, Yankee Spy: The True Story of Elizabeth Van Lew, a Union Agent in the Heart of the Confederacy*. New York: Oxford University Press, 2003.

Washington, Versalle F. *Eagles on Their Buttons: A Black Infantry Regiment in the Civil War*. Columbia: University of Missouri Press, 1999.

Wert, Jeffry D. *From Winchester to Cedar Creek: The Shenandoah Campaign of 1864*. Mechanicsburg, PA: Stackpole Books, 1997.

Westwood, Howard C. *Black Troops, White Commanders, and Freedmen during the Civil War*. Carbondale: Southern Illinois University Press, 1992.

Williams, George W. *A History of the Negro Troops in the War of the Rebellion, 1861–1865*. New York: Harper & Brothers, 1888.

Wilson, Joseph T. *The Black Phalanx: A History of the Negro Soldiers of the United States in the Wars of 1775–1812, 1861–'65*. Hartford, CT: American Publishing Company, 1890.

———. *Voice of a New Race: Original Selections of Poems with a Trilogy and Oration*. Hampton, VA: Normal School Steam Press, 1882.

Winkler, Donald H. *Stealing Secrets: How a Few Daring Women Deceived Generals, Impacted Battles, and Altered the Course of the Civil War*. Naperville, IL: Cumberland House, 2010.

INDEX

About the Author

J ames S. Price is a Civil War historian, blogger and educator who specializes in the history of African American Union soldiers. He has worked for many Civil War sites and museums, including Petersburg National Battlefield, Pamplin Historical Park and the American Civil War Center at historic Tredegar. In 2009, he received his MA in military history from Norwich University. For the past three years, he has dedicated himself to the study of the Battle of New Market Heights and has sought to raise awareness of this important battle by leading specialized tours of the preserved portions of the battlefield, lecturing throughout the metro Richmond area on the topic and writing about different aspects of the battle on his weblog, the Sable Arm: A Blog Dedicated to the United States Colored Troops of the Civil War Era (http://sablearm.blogspot.com). It is his hope that by raising public awareness of the services rendered by United States Colored Troops, the fields on which they fought will be preserved for future generations.

Visit us at
www.historypress.net